THE GRANGER RAILROADS OF WISCONSIN

THE GRANGER RAILROADS OF WISCONSIN

WHEN MIDWESTERN FARMERS FOUGHT BIG INDUSTRY

DANIEL FAAS

THE History PRESS

Published by The History Press
An imprint of Arcadia Publishing
Charleston, SC
www.historypress.com

First published 2025

Manufactured in the United States

ISBN 9781467157827

Library of Congress Control Number: 2025931157

To my wife, who has been my rock as I have chased the dream of writing my first book, and to my children, whose curiosity keeps me searching and learning every day.

CONTENTS

INTRODUCTION

In rural Sauk County, nestled into the driftless region of Southwest Wisconsin, lies a 22-mile ribbon of limestone gravel. This trail, dubbed the 400 State Trail, is a multiuse running, walking, horseback riding and cycling route, part of the greater network of state trails throughout Wisconsin. The trail is relatively flat and straight, for much of its length follows the bucolic Baraboo River, which at 120 miles is the longest river in the nation to be freed of the confining influences of its eleven man-made dams. Riding the "400" is a common pastime for those residing in the numerous small cities and towns along its length. The trail has even played host to epic endurance events such as the Ride Across Wisconsin, a 230-mile ride that takes participants from the Mississippi to the shores of Lake Michigan. In some communities along the 400 trail, the route has brought revitalization through an influx of bikers and hikers to downtowns that had seen a decline in business through the last half of the twentieth century and into the twenty-first.

However, the 400 is more than just a recreational rail, it is the remnant of a once-powerful railroad empire that held the Midwest, and even the nation, in its grip. Founded in 1859, the Chicago and North Western Railroad (CNW) began laying track across the burgeoning states of Wisconsin, Minnesota, Iowa and Illinois, among many others. One of the flagship routes of the CNW during the early twentieth century was its 400 services, one of the fastest passenger routes in the world when it was running. The route gained its moniker from the company's claim that the train covered 400 miles in 400 minutes, station stops included, as it ran from Chicago to St.

Paul, Minnesota, traversing much of the state of Wisconsin in the process. With speeds approaching 110 miles per hour in certain stretches, the 400 trains became a hit through the 1930s, alongside other speedy passenger services offered by famous railroads such as the Milwaukee Road, Chicago, Burlington and Quincy, as well as the Rock Island Route.

Railroad construction through the first half of the nineteenth century was a start-and-stop affair, never totaling more than 1,200 miles in any calendar year. Much of this expansion occurred in the eastern portions of the United States, where population and business made construction routes a more profitable venture. However, from 1850, except for a slight pause during the Civil War, railroad construction boomed. Construction would peak in 1887 with a staggering 13,081 miles laid and would not fall below 1,500 miles per year until 1915. The railways of the upper Midwest benefited greatly from manifest destiny's westward drive and the opening of new lands in the unsettled plains states.

One of the great driving forces of the exodus from the East was the Homestead Act. Enacted in 1862, this act of the Thirty-Seventh Congress of the United States provided 160 acres of federally held land to anyone willing to farm the land they were given. By 1890, over 390,000 Americans had taken advantage of the act, netting nearly 48 million acres of land throughout the West. These farms became the beating heart of the agricultural economy and needed access to markets in the East for their various products. From the earliest days of settlement in the West, one of the primary modes of transporting farm goods was by ship. The Mississippi River and its tributaries featured ubiquitous paddle steamers carrying passengers and goods up and down the mighty corridor. Elsewhere, the Great Lakes provided a vital lifeline for farmers, as between 1831 and 1888, wheat was the most abundant bulk shipping item carried to ports on the East Coast via the Great Lakes.

Yet the march of progress continued, and just as the paddle steamers of the East Coast canals and Midwest rivers were finding their stride, a new mode of transportation came on the scene, the railroad. Beginning in the mid-1840s, nearly concurrent with the addition of Wisconsin and Iowa to the union, railroads began to incorporate in the new territories, emanating from the prosperous industrial centers of Milwaukee and Chicago. While the expansion of these young roads was slow at first, and often came in starts and fits, their inevitable expansion into the farming and mining communities of the upper Midwest brought with them a new avenue of access to eastern markets. No longer did farmers need to transport their crops by land to ports on the Mississippi such as La Crosse, St. Paul or Duluth; a local grain elevator could deposit their harvests directly to railcars destined for the points east. As the railroads began to turn a profit, their value to the growing economy became apparent and investments from around the nation and even abroad multiplied. Quickly, investments began to flood into the coffers of the railroads. By the 1850s and into the years just before the Civil War, construction began an upward trend that would continue for years to come, connecting small towns across the Midwest and bringing the ends of the country closer together.

By the early part of the twentieth century, a quartet of railways, including the CNW, home to the 400 route, held sway over much of the passenger and freight traffic of the upper Midwest. These railways were the Chicago, Milwaukee, St. Paul and Pacific Railroad, often called the Milwaukee Road; the Chicago, Burlington and Quincy Railroad; the Chicago and North Western Railroad; and the Chicago, Rock Island and Pacific Railroad. These four railroads all found their genesis in the early days of railroad construction in the United States, some of them even being founded before the states they would later come to dominate.

However, the success of these railroads, from modest beginnings in the mid-nineteenth century to having 36,117 miles of rail by the eve of World War II, was at one point in their history very much in doubt. A growing movement among farmers of the Midwest in the years just after the Civil War called the National Grange of the Order of Patrons of Husbandry was at the center of a move to rein in the railroads through the use of legislation. The National Grange was concerned that the railroads were near to a monopoly and that their unfair policies were affecting the livelihood of farmers throughout the nation.

The primary concern of the farmers of the upper Midwest was perceived dishonesty in the method by which the railroads and, by extension, the grain elevators, set freight rates. The major markets for farm goods were in the populated cities of the Eastern Seaboard. This left the farmers at the mercy of the railroads when it came to shipping. Many farmers felt they were forced into accepting whichever rates the railroads were charging, and they also saw the high prices their crops were fetching once they arrived in the markets in the East. Around the same time, in 1873, a financial collapse in Europe led to a series of U.S. bank failures and a resultant depression in the United States popularly referred to as the Panic of 1873.

As the membership in the National Grange exploded during the 1870s, the otherwise fraternal organization took on a distinctly political nature. The

Grange began to agitate for legislation that would support farmers and rein in the railroads. Nowhere was this influence so acutely felt than in the states of Wisconsin, Minnesota, Iowa and Illinois. Throughout these four states, radical new legislation was passed, thanks in no small part to the Grange's influence in electing candidates friendly to the cause of the farmers. Of the various laws, the strictest, Potters Law in Wisconsin, became an early harbinger of populist reforms that would characterize the latter years of the nineteenth century across the nation.

The outcry from railroads was immediate and overwhelming. Railroad managers claimed these new "Granger Laws" were tantamount to illegal confiscation of property due to the deleterious effects they would have on the ability of the railroads to conduct their businesses. Some railroads flatly refused to comply until the courts could satisfy their constitutional concerns. In the landmark case of *Munn v. Illinois*, the Supreme Court famously ruled that private businesses that served the public interest could indeed be regulated by the states using their police powers, ushering in the age of business regulation.

Nevertheless, the immediate effect of Potters Law in Wisconsin was short-lived, as within two years, the state legislature repealed the controversial railroad controls. It also seemed another Illinois court case would hand the railroads back their legal advantages. In *Wabash v. Illinois*, the court found that Illinois could not dictate rates on the Wabash Road, as the majority of the traffic was inter-, rather than intrastate traffic. It would not take long, however, for the federal government to step into the limelight as the new arbiter of fair business practices. This time, Congress relied on the Constitution's commerce clause to introduce a new bill, the Interstate Commerce Act.

Despite these new controls, over the next fifty years, the railroads, especially the Granger Railroads, would go from strength to strength. By 1916, track mileage in the United States had reached its peak, and by 1920, railroad employment had peaked at over 1.8 million workers. To say that rail was a dominant force in the United States would have been a vast understatement. However, developments in the United States and around the world would soon, alongside ICC's glacial pace of regulation, bring about the beginning of the end of the rail age.

The first disaster to strike the railroads was the Great Depression. Following the stock market crash of 1929 as well as an interconnected web of global tariffs, a global depression hit the labor and business markets of the United States. By 1941, a devastatingly large portion of rail miles in the

United States had entered receivership, totaling 74,214 miles according to the ICC. At its peak during the Great Depression, unemployment within the United States hit 25 percent. Falling consumer spending coupled with a disastrous drought and the ensuing Dust Bowl on the plains devastated the agricultural industry; the railroads felt the squeeze as revenues fell by nearly half during the Great Depression.

By the 1930s, the forces of modernization were also beginning to press on the railroads, especially those smaller railroads without the resources of the larger national carriers. Diesel locomotives began supplanting steam power as the most efficient means of transporting goods. Faced with fleets of obsolete steam engines, many managers struggled to find resources during the Great Depression and into World War II to renew their fleets and save soaring overhead costs. At the same time, diesel engines made their way into another industry—trucking. The move toward trucks as a method of shipping freight grew steadily in the early twentieth century as engine technology grew stronger and more reliable. Coupled with the burgeoning interstate highway system in the years following the Second World War, trucking was becoming the dominant way to ship goods across the continental United States, while personal cars were the preferred mode for passengers.

As railroads were struggling to compete with trucks and replace the steam engines of old with new and sleek diesel-electric engines, another force compounded their efforts. The ICC held sway over maximum and minimum rates that the railroads could charge, often holding bulk goods like grain from the Midwest at a lower rate than manufactured goods. These rates had the effect of driving manufacturing toward the trucks that plied the expanding network of roads throughout the nation. Furthermore, rate schedules often held rates between two points at a nearly identical cost regardless of the costs incurred by one railroad over another. Passenger travel had been declining for years as well, but ICC regulations also required roads to maintain these often unprofitable routes, further hurting their bottom lines.

As the calendar continued to turn, the expansion of air travel and road travel meant further declines in passenger revenue, and by the 1970s, railroads were incurring a total loss of nearly $200 million per year. The federal government again stepped in and nationalized passenger travel within the United States by creating Amtrak to relieve the freight roads of their passenger duties. However, many railroads continued to struggle, and by the 1980s, many managers faced a choice: abandon entire lines or merge with another railroad company to stay afloat. As the ICC and its system of outdated regulations and rate controls became untenable, new laws, such as the Staggers Act, took their place, vastly reorganizing how the federal government regulated the rails.

By the mid-1990s, none of the Granger Railroads remained. Some, such as the Milwaukee Road and CNW, faded into obscurity, casting off large portions of their network before finally being absorbed. Others were incorporated through mergers into the new mega-railroads of the twenty-first century like the Chicago Burlington and Quincy, now part of BNSF. However, the dissolution of the railroads left many questions unanswered. What to do with the vast tracts of land the federal government had given many of the railroads as early as the 1850s? How to handle abandoned railroad rights-of-way? What, if any, cautionary tales can be gleaned from the nearly century-long regulatory experiment of the Granger Laws and later the ICC?

This book, beyond providing a modern history of the story of the National Grange and their crusade against the railroads to which they would lend their name, hopes to answer these questions. The legacy of the Granger Railroads goes far beyond bike trails and abandoned railway rights-of-way. The economic landscape of the Midwest and by extension the entire United States is inexorably linked to those farmers who in 1870 organized to air their grievances. To a great extent, the development of the western states, the development of agriculture in the Midwest and modern transportation infrastructure are at the heart of this discussion. Lastly, how did this development hamstring the United States when it came to modern passenger rail travel, leaving the United States decades behind other Asian and European nations when it comes to efficient high-speed rail?

This book attempts to answer all these questions and lay out a compelling narrative about the rise, dominance and later fall of the railroad industry in the United States and its link to a largely forgotten farmers organization. However, this work also attempts to give a voice to the independent farmers who banded together, using the tools of democracy at their disposal, to attempt to take on the mega-corporations of their time. At its heart, the story of the Granger Railroads is a story of America, a constant tug-of-war between economic progress and the rights of the people at large. There is much we can learn and apply in the twenty-first century from this century-and-a-half-old struggle.

1

LAND GRANTS, SPECULATION AND THE RISE OF THE EARLY RAILROADS

The story of the American rail industry begins, as many stories in the collective history of this nation, on the East Coast. In February 1827, the first charter for an American railroad was granted to connect the city of Baltimore to the Ohio River. Construction began the next year, and the first chartered railroad was operational. The B&O, as it would later and more famously be referred to, became a cornerstone of the rail industry in the United States. The B&O hauled much of its freight as coal from the Allegheny Mountains of western Pennsylvania. The B&O became such an icon of American business that it would even be immortalized in the Parker Brothers game Monopoly, alongside other famous East Coast rail lines such as the Reading and Pennsylvania Railroads.

While the B&O would not reach its Ohio River terminus until 1852, the race between rail transport and canal or river transport had begun, sparking a shipping rivalry that would continue into the twentieth century. As early as the fall of 1827, shortly after the incorporation of the B&O but before any track had yet to be laid, the question of rail transport's advantage over canals such as the recently completed Erie Canal was entering the public consciousness. An article in the *Western Carolinian* titled "Internal Improvement" discussed several reasons that the railroads were as good or better than the canals, which the author states had previously been "the cheapest means of communication and conveyance through the interior of a country." The reasons cited were numerous, including the cost per mile of a railroad compared to canals, the ability to transport a similar amount of goods for a similar amount of energy and the maintenance costs of railroads compared to canals. Perhaps most importantly, canals require routes that have access to water and, as a result, need to be much longer than a rail route between the same two points in many cases and are nearly impossible in other cases.

While those in the public were busy discussing the relative efficacy of railroads and canals as a means of mass transport, in the greater economy, the overall necessity of mass transport was becoming apparent. The nation was growing, both in terms of population and area. In 1800, the U.S. territory stretched only as far as the Mississippi River and totaled just over 5 million inhabitants. By 1830, the territorial size of the United States had nearly doubled, and the population had nearly tripled to 12.8 million. Much of this growth was happening in the "West," as it was known at the time, with states like Ohio, Indiana, Illinois, Missouri and Michigan joining the union, among others.

First stone laid on the B&O Railroad. *Library of Congress.*

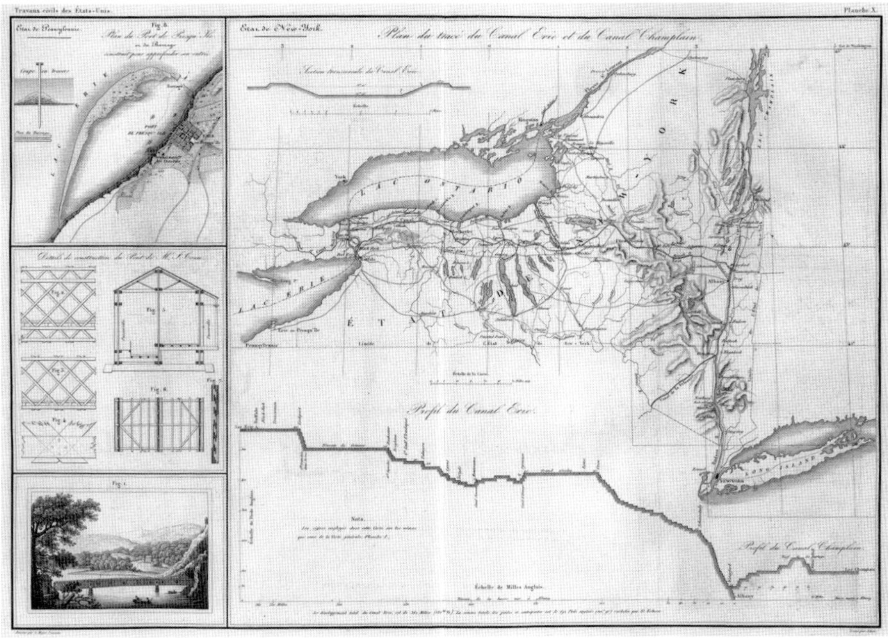

Erie Canal Map. *David Rumsey Map Archive.*

A system of canals was one of the first attempts at creating a network to move goods and people between the heavily populated East Coast cities and the quickly growing interior. These initial efforts were constrained by many factors, most prominently a lack of funds and technology necessary to build canals and the locks needed to traverse the elevations required by the routes that were dictated by the geography of the eastern half of the United States. Perhaps the most successful canal of this early period in U.S. history was the Erie Canal. This canal, connecting the Hudson River to Lake Erie, opened the Great Lakes coastline to the important markets of the East Coast and New York Harbor. The importance of the Erie Canal to New York State must be recognized: the cost of shipping goods through the canal was 90 percent cheaper than comparable rates to ship by wagon across the rugged interior. Throughout much of New York's history, population growth was also tied geographically to the canal's route; even in a modern post-canal economic landscape, nearly 80 percent of the population of New York State lives within twenty-five miles of the canal.

The sudden outgrowth of canal building in the United States led to an era rather uncreatively dubbed the Canal Era, which lasted until 1850, when the railroads usurped the canals as the primary means of moving goods and people around the United States. As the nation pushed its frontiers farther west, a new water corridor became vital to the livelihood of the new midwestern states, the Mississippi River. As more and more settlers moved west, cities began to grow along the Mississippi River and Great Lakes coast, one of the most important of these upstart cities being Chicago, Illinois. In 1833, Chicago was a small town of only slightly more than three hundred residents, but the creation of a new canal project soon thrust Chicago into the forefront of the economic and population growth that took the nation by storm in the nineteenth century.

Beginning in 1836, a canal was dug from Lake Michigan at Chicago to the Illinois River, to gain shipping access to the Mississippi. With its completion in 1848, the Illinois and Michigan Canal (I&M) made it possible to travel from growing Midwest cities like St. Louis and Chicago to New York City by way of the Great Lakes and the Erie Canal. The transfer time for shipping goods to New York was cut by more than half, down to twelve days from the previous thirty to forty days it took by shipping through the Ohio River valley. This increased access to the Midwest also brought a windfall for farmers, who were now more able to ship excess agricultural goods to the increasingly hungry cities on the East Coast. In the following years, Chicago grew in leaps and bounds. By 1850, the city was home to thirty thousand residents, and a further eighty thousand would flock to the city by 1860.

With the growth of Chicago and its geographic location on the coast of Lake Michigan and with water access to the Mississippi, Chicago quickly became the crossroads of America. To cope with the new demand for shipping products to the East Coast, shipbuilding soon became a booming industry in the city. The first ship built in the city was the *Clarissa*, completed in 1835, and in the ensuing decade, another eighty ships were produced by Chicago shipyards. However, the completion of the I&M Canal was nearly rendered moot by geographic issues facing the harbor front in Chicago, illustrating the complexities and costs associated with canal infrastructure. A frugal President James Polk vetoed a federal bill that would have provided funds to expand and dredge the harbor, leaving the issue to be funded independently by the city of Chicago. Polk reasoned, in a message regarding his controversial decision, that the Constitution did not provide for improvements that were internal to the various states. This narrow view of the Constitution's provisions for the federal government to manage commerce would change dramatically over the next thirty years but at the time demonstrated the hesitance of the federal government to directly regulate commerce.

Concurrent with the construction of the I&M Canal, farther north in the growing Wisconsin Territory, another canal hoped to mirror the success of the I&M. In south-central Wisconsin, a thin strip of land that measured only slightly more than two miles separated the Fox River with its Lake Michigan terminus and the Wisconsin River as it wound its way down to the Mississippi. The area had since the fur trapping days been used as a site where trappers beached and then moved their canoes overland from one river to the other. The site held such importance that in 1828, the federal government erected Fort Winnebago at the site of the portage, the centerpiece in a string of forts along the Fox and Wisconsin Rivers. This movement, called a *portage* in the native language of the early French fur trappers, gave the town and later canal its name.

Construction of the Portage Canal began in 1837 and would not be completed for commercial travel until 1876, well beyond the prime years of the Canal Era and into the dominance of the railroads as far as transportation was concerned. However, the fact that it was completed at all for commercial travel speaks to the value that many in the Midwest saw in shipping connections to the great ports of the South and East Coast. By the middle of the nineteenth century, the new state of Wisconsin was home to growing agricultural and mining regions. The lead deposits of Southwest Wisconsin were, for a time, the most prosperous in the world, making up half the national output for a time. Copper mining in the Upper Peninsula of Michigan and iron mining in northern Minnesota all required a constant supply of resources to build up mines and infrastructure as well as a constant outflow of ore to markets. The fact that the federal government, through the Army Corps of Engineers, would complete a project such as the Portage Canal in the face of growing competition from the railroads speaks to the volume of commerce that was emanating from these new and growing states.

However, economics soon rendered the canals subservient to the railroads in their quest to be the primary form of overland transportation in the United States. The overall costs of shipping via rail in the early years of the railroads did not initially prove to be advantageous when compared to the canals. Canals enjoyed significant cost savings in the early part of the nineteenth century; in some cases, overland turnpike travel could cost nearly four times as much per ton as the canals, and the advantage to canals only improved as technology continued to advance. In terms of

The Portage Canal in Portage, Wisconsin. *Wisconsin Historical Society.*

transportation times, the canals also significantly reduced overland travel times within the expanding western frontier. According to George Rodgers Taylor in his work *The Transportation Revolution*, the canals were able to cut nearly thirty days off of the overall travel time between Cincinnati and New York. However, once rail connections were created, the travel time fell even further. Despite the relatively higher cost of transport, around two dollars a mile per ton compared with only one dollar for canal travel, the reduction in time was more than twenty days, bottoming out at around six to eight days on the railroads.

Before there were even any rail connections to the East Coast, the first railroads were being incorporated in the Midwest. Beginning in 1838, the first railroad in the state of Illinois also became the first operational road in what would eventually become the Granger States. The Northern Cross Railroad was, in its earliest forms, a short line that ran a handful of miles from Meredosia to Springfield, Illinois. Over the ensuing years, the state funded extensions that would see the line run across the state from the Illinois River to the Mississippi River, mirroring much of the same route that ships took along the I&M Canal. In the late 1840s, the state sold off the railroad to a private individual, creating a charter for the Sangamon and Morgan Railroad, itself later absorbed into the Wabash Railway, which would later prove to be a key player in the fight for railroad regulation. However, the creation of a profitable railroad at the same time and nearly the same location as a successful canal proved that railroads could be successful in the western states and opened up a floodgate of railroad speculation in the Midwest.

The first of the four "Granger Railroads," as they were known later in their life, owing to the grassroots agrarian movement that later challenged their supremacy, was founded in 1847. In a February 16 article appearing in the *Milwaukee Daily Sentinel*, sandwiched between another railroad charter for the Fond du Lac and Beaver Dam Railroad and charters for various churches throughout the state, the following appeared: "and a bill to incorporate the Milwaukee and Waukesha R.R." The article goes on to discuss how the charter was once defeated by the state legislature but narrowly passed in a second vote. While the start to what would later be known as the Milwaukee Road was somewhat inauspicious, the company went on to be one of the most extensive and influential of the Granger Roads. By November 1847, the railroad had appointed Lemuel W. Weeks

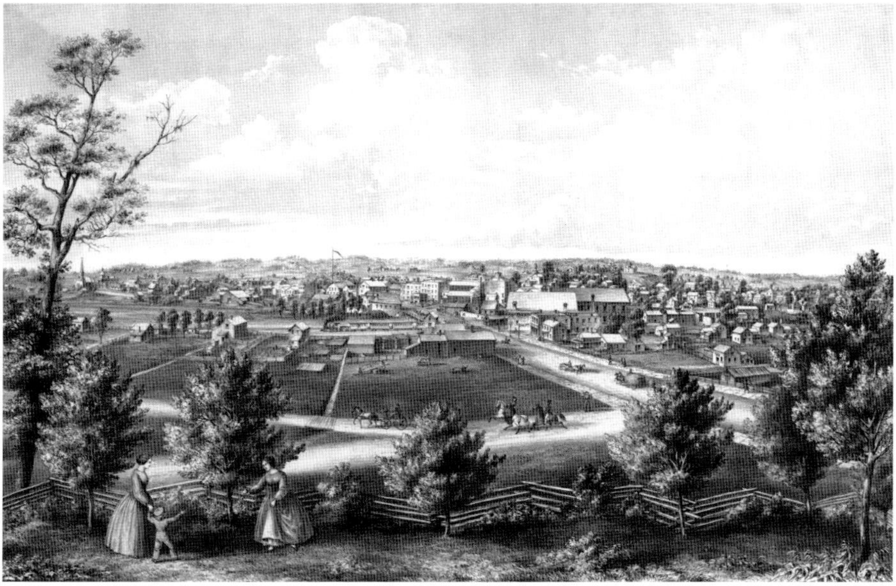

Waukesha Railroad engraving. *Library of Congress.*

as the president of the railroad's board and began to make plans for stock sales in Milwaukee and Waukesha.

In the years before the incorporation of Wisconsin as the thirtieth state, the area around Milwaukee and Waukesha in southeastern Wisconsin saw a tremendous amount of growth; the population of Milwaukee doubled from 1846 to 1850 alone. This rapid growth, much like Chicago, made Milwaukee a center for commerce in the coming years. The first rail operations of the Milwaukee and Waukesha, renamed the Milwaukee and Mississippi by this point as the result of a new charter that gave the railroad a route to the Mississippi River through Grant County, occurred in November 1850, some three years after the incorporation of the railroad. In a ceremonial first ride, many local dignitaries, including Solomon Juneau, the first white settler of Milwaukee, were given a ride from Milwaukee to Wauwatosa, a trip of approximately seven miles, which,

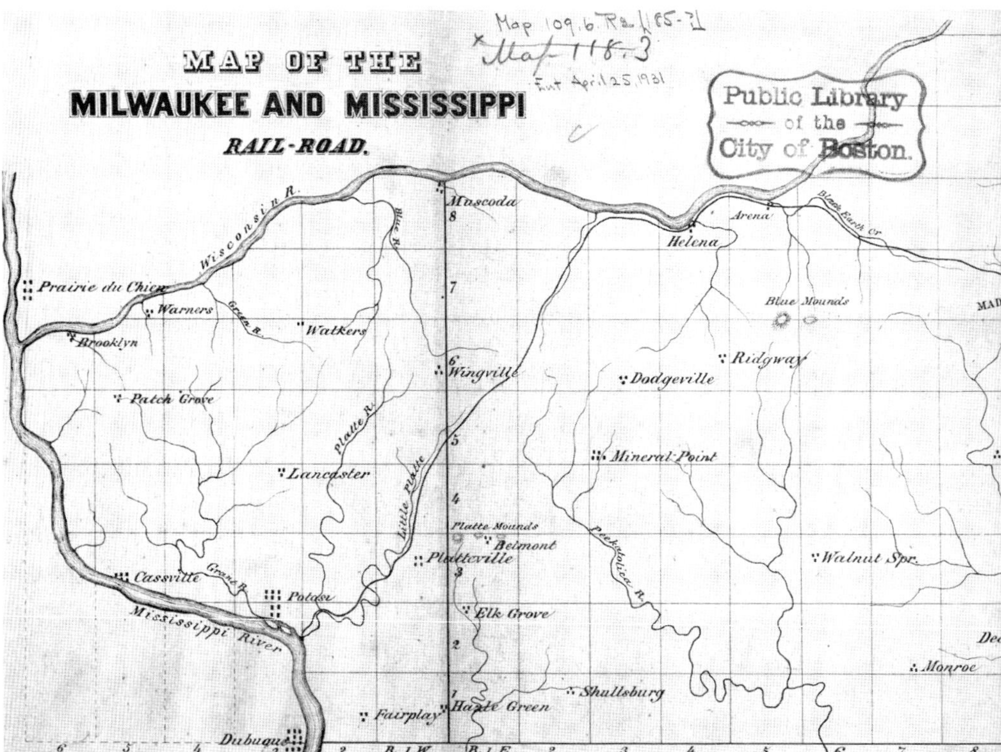

as the *Telegraph Courier* reported, "in *twelve* minutes brought up at Spurr's Tavern in Wauwatosa, going at the rate of 30 miles per hour, without any special effort." The fact that the area's first white settler was now riding the state's first railroad from a city of some twenty-two thousand inhabitants speaks to the rapid settlement and industrialization that characterized the middle part of the nineteenth century for Wisconsin, the Midwest and the nation as a whole.

As the 1850s rolled on, the Milwaukee and Mississippi Railroad continued its march toward the Mississippi River, finally reaching the opposite coast of Wisconsin on April 15, 1857, at Prairie Du Chien. The trip was problem-free, taking ten and a half hours according to an article in the *Wisconsin State Journal* detailing the festivities. Having been renamed the Milwaukee and Mississippi (M&M) in 1855, the railroad had reached its namesake goal. However, there was much discussion over the circuitous

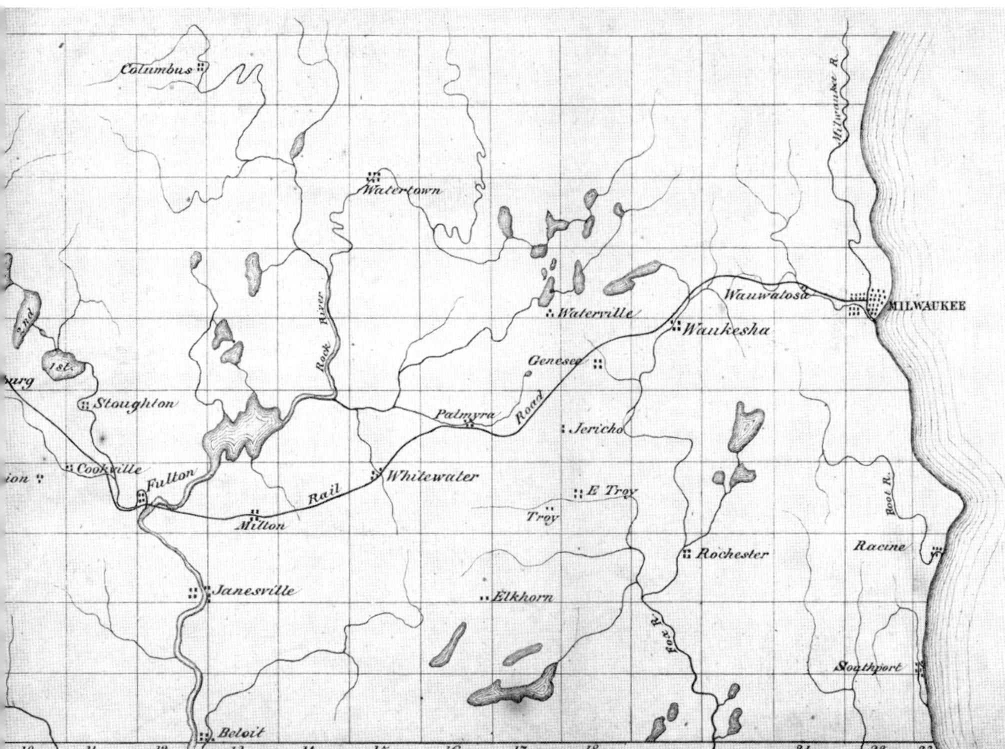

Map of the Milwaukee and Mississippi Railroad, 1857. *Norman B. Leventhal Map & Education Center at the Boston Public Library.*

course used by the road. In a February 1857 article in the *Wisconsin Journal*, a Mr. Sweat, speaking on opposition to a road parallel to the M&M, said any opposition would be fatal, as nearly any railroad in the state would be parallel to at least some portion of the M&M.

The M&M reached Prairie Du Chien at a difficult time, as the panic of 1857 struck the United States in September. The cascading financial crisis affected the fledgling railroad industry. Compounding issues such as reduced access to capital as a result of bank failures in the East along with low grain prices meant that the western railroads, which depended heavily on agricultural shipments, experienced significant financial hardships, and the M&M was not immune. As the roads began to fail, farmers, many of whom had mortgaged their farms to buy stock in the railroads, found their stock worthless. On January 12, 1859, the *Racine Journal* reported that nearly $700,000 of stock had been raised by farmer mortgages for the M&M alone and $2.7 million in total, with little value having been added, especially as roads began to falter during the years of the panic. The M&M entered receivership, only to be purchased in a mortgage sale on January 18, 1861, emerging from the sale as the Milwaukee and Prairie du Chien Railroad (M&PdC). The M&PdC emerged from its mortgage sale in strength. By July 1861, reports in the *Janesville Daily Gazette* showed that the M&PdC was receiving nearly $140,000 a month in income primarily through freight, both a sign of the future of the railroad and its reliance on agriculture as well as the renewed financial strength of the railroad only months after their sale. The road was consistently busy throughout the early part of 1861. On June 12, an article in the *North Iowa Times* reported that fifty freight cars were making the journey from Prairie du Chien to Milwaukee per day.

By 1867, the M&PdC had expanded through consolidation to lands farther north and west. In 1867, the road acquired the McGregor and Western Railroads as well as the Minnesota Central Railroads, emerging with a new name: the Milwaukee and St. Paul Railroad, after a long-debated merger with the Milwaukee and St. Paul Railroad, formerly known as the La Crosse and Milwaukee. With these purchases, the road now connected Milwaukee to the capital city of Minnesota by way of northeastern Iowa. Within seven years, the road saw yet another name change, ultimately resulting in the name that would last on into the late twentieth century. On February 7, 1874, at a board meeting of Milwaukee and St. Paul, the board voted to amend the name of the company to Chicago, Milwaukee and St. Paul. The road had been informally referred

Milwaukee and Prairie du Chien Locomotive 1848. *Milwaukee Public Library—Milwaukee Road Archives.*

to as the Chicago, Milwaukee and St. Paul (CM&SP) since completing its line to Chicago in 1873, now linking the three great cities of Illinois, Wisconsin and Minnesota together. The CM&SP kept this official name for much of the rest of its history, but it was more popularly known by its unofficial moniker, the Milwaukee Road.

As the Milwaukee Road was making rapid progress toward extending its routes into the prairies of western Minnesota, a second of the Granger Roads was just finding its feet as well. While the aforementioned Northern Cross may have begun service in 1838, another railroad incorporated a year earlier served as the genesis for what would become the Chicago and North Western Railroad. In January 1836, the State of Illinois granted a charter for the Galena and Chicago Union Railroad (G&CU). This road was meant to extend east from Chicago toward the Mississippi River border and beyond. It was not until 1848 however, that rail service began on this line. There was considerable controversy over the completion of the Chicago and Galena, however, as many industrialists in St. Louis worried that the completion of the Chicago and Galena might cut into their profits in the midst of the ongoing lead boom in and around the city. Galena's location abreast the Mississippi River made shipping by steamboat an easy and profitable affair, and those in St. Louis likely worried that a direct route to the Chicago area might mean being cut out of the trade altogether.

By 1854, the Galena and Chicago had reached the goal of connecting the lead mining city to Chicago and later continued its lines farther west into another of the new midwestern states, Iowa. In a November 1862 notice to shareholders from the board of the G&CU found in the *Wisconsin State Register*, it was noted that the G&CU had obtained leases over the Chicago, Iowa and Nebraska Railroad as well as the Cedar Rapids and Missouri Railroads, giving the G&CU a line that could connect the city of Chicago all the way to the western border of Iowa. As stated in the article, the board sold these moves to shareholders as "desiring to maintain

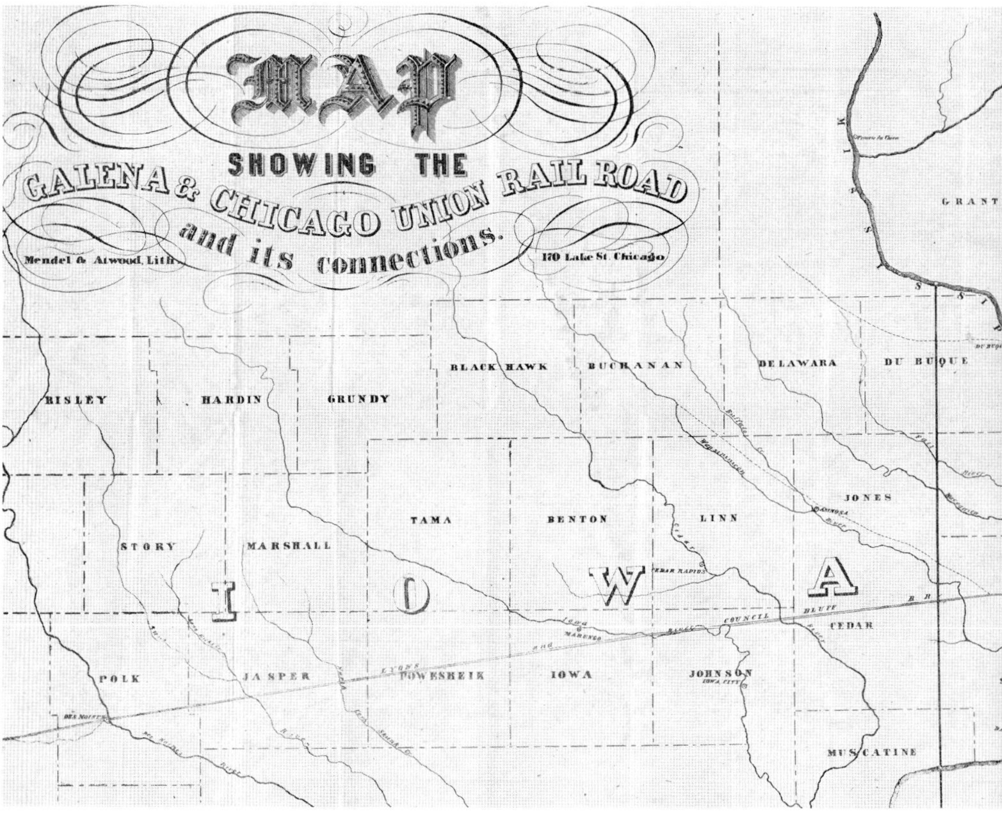

the present amount of revenues" in the face of what they called the "construction of rival lines of railroad in Northern Illinois and Southern Wisconsin." This connection gave the G&CU a unique ability to serve the burgeoning grain growing territories in Iowa to supplement their mineral shipments from Galena.

Meanwhile, another constituent railroad that would later become a part of the CNW was finding its origin as well. On May 11, 1853, the *Weekly Wisconsin* reported that the City of Milwaukee approved an $80,000 loan to the Milwaukee and Watertown Railway to commence operations on its line between the two cities, as well as a $40,000 loan to the Watertown and Berlin Railroad. The fact the city was willing to lay out such large sums of money to these fledgling companies is another illustration of the value seen in bringing rail service to the interior of the state and the economic return the city envisioned resulting from their completion.

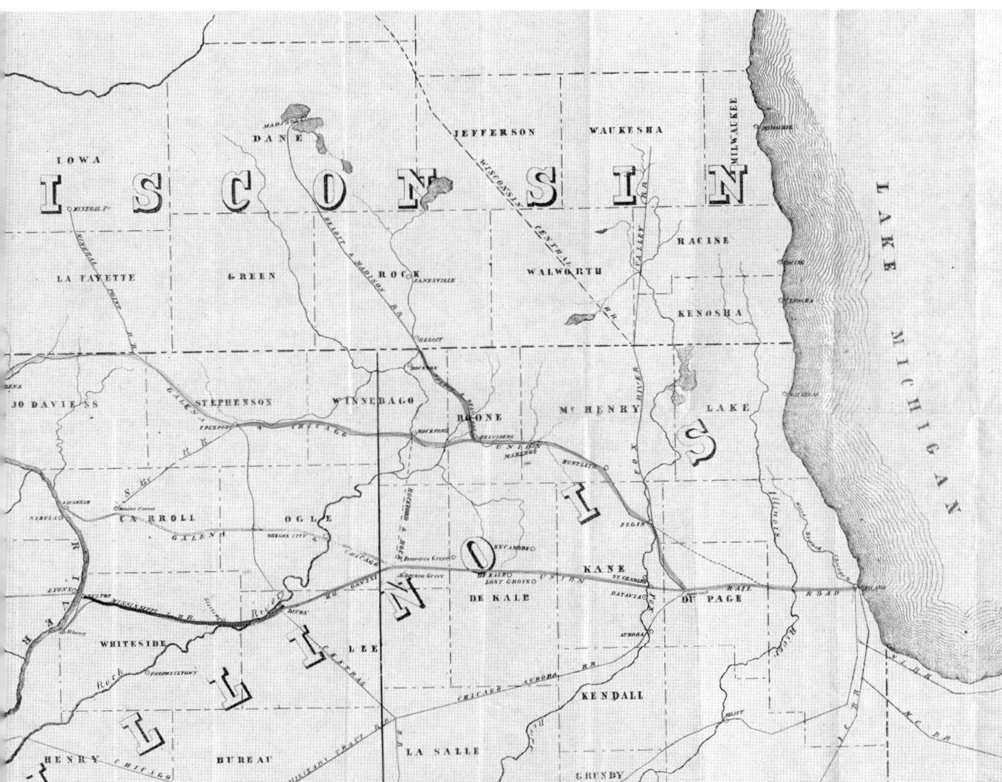

Map of the Galena & Chicago Union Railroad, 1853. *Yale University Library*.

The value was not lost on the inhabitants of the state either. In an article from the *Watertown Chronicle* in January 1853, the economic effect of the Milwaukee and Waukesha Railway was estimated to "add 25 to 40 percent to the value of their products." This estimate was made based on the increase in farm product values due to the recently completed Milwaukee and Mississippi Railroad and the economic effect for farmers being served by that line. By November 1854, track had been laid and was approaching its opening. The first stretch of track ran on Milwaukee and Mississippi lines from Watertown for fourteen miles and then continued on its own track the rest of the way to Hartland, Wisconsin, according to the *Sauk County Standard*. Within a year, the railroad had further pushed the terminus of the line to Oconomowoc, Wisconsin, another nine miles farther east. By the end of 1855, the railroad was profitably running to its originally intended destination at Watertown and doing such business that by January 1856, it was being reported that new freight houses were being built and were "immediately necessary."

However, a competing road soon entered the fray, as reported in the *Waukesha Plaindealer*, buying up the Milwaukee and Watertown Railroad in September 1856. The Milwaukee and La Crosse Railroad, chartered only a few years earlier, would operate the Milwaukee and Watertown as its Watertown division for another two years. Within another year of the purchase by the Milwaukee and La Crosse, in March 1857, it was being reported that the Milwaukee and Watertown, now referred to as the Milwaukee, Watertown and Madison, was hoping to sell securities to extend its terminus to the state capital, an estimated outlay of some $1 million. However, in March 1858, the Milwaukee and La Crosse sold off its stake in the Milwaukee and Watertown to the Madison, Fond du Lac and Michigan Railroad, to much distress in Watertown.

The resultant railroad, the Chicago, St. Paul and Fond du Lac, continued operations into 1859, when, on June 7, the board of directors sold their stake to new proprietors and, in doing so, created the Chicago and North Western Railroad. Within a few years, the Chicago and North Western swallowed up the Galena and Chicago Union Railroad as well. Between 1864 and 1865, a series of moves by the board of the Galena and Chicago Union as well as the Chicago and North Western ended in the CNW taking control of the original Chicago railroad.

The third of the Granger Railroads to find its foundations was the Chicago, Rock Island and Pacific Railroad. The originator road of the Chicago, Rock Island and Pacific was the Rock Island and La Salle

Railroad, its charter being approved by the Illinois legislature in February 1847. Funding was scarce, however, and the Rock Island and La Salle was forced to sell subscriptions of stock to the general public. However, by 1850, it was clear the public was excited about a railway, similar to the sentiment that had swept rural Wisconsin, and by November 1850, $300,000 had been raised and the road was on its way to being realized. Only a few months later, in March 1851, the Rock Island and La Salle was reincorporated as the Chicago and Rock Island Railroad. In October 1851, with much fanfare, construction finally began, starting in Joliet, Illinois. One editorial in the *Belvidere Standard* reported the occasion was celebrated by a circus band, the firing of a cannon and three cheers for the railroad. By the end of October 1852, more than forty miles of track had been completed and trains were regularly running between Chicago and Joliet. The line would not reach its namesake terminus of Rock Island until the spring of 1854, when a first-class ticket from Chicago to Rock Island cost five dollars.

The incorporators of the Chicago and Rock Island, buoyed by the success of the line, looked westward. In February 1853, they incorporated Iowa's first railroad, the Mississippi and Missouri (M&M). The road hoped to connect the two great rivers of the state of Iowa, the Mississippi and Missouri Rivers, between Davenport and Council Bluffs. On September 1, the railroad broke ground in Davenport, Iowa. With many of these original railroads, there is much evidence that the settlers and the cities of these regions were heavily invested in bringing a rail connection to their town. In Davenport, the origination point for the M&M, a successful vote was held in the city asking citizens whether or not $75,000 of the city budget should go toward subscriptions to the railroad, a sizeable portion of the city surplus at the time.

However, starting a railroad was not always a guarantee of financial success in the early days. Failed roads and mergers between competing roads were common in the first few decades of rail construction. While local governments were getting their feet wet helping fund railroads, the federal government had, until 1852, generally stayed out of regulating the railroads. Yet all of that changed in 1852, when the federal government began to use one of its most considerable resources to boost the construction of railroads in the ever-expanding frontier in the West—land. In most cases, the federal government ceded the land to the state in which the railroad was to be built and left it to the authority of the state to determine the exact route and company to build the railway. While the economic benefit provided value in and of itself, the federal government was also able to use the land grant roads for postal service at a rate dictated by Congress, essentially outsourcing mail-carrying infrastructure at little to no cost. Between 1850 and 1870, nearly 7 percent of all of the land within the United States was granted to railroads to raise funds and provide a right-of-way for a new track. The effect on railroads was immediately felt. In 1854, a new peak of rail construction occurred in the United States, with over three thousand miles being laid in that year alone.

One benefactor of land grants was indeed the M&M Railroad. On April 12, 1852, Congress passed a bill granting large portions of federally held land in Iowa to be used for two routes. One route would stretch from Dubuque to Keokuk, Iowa, on a roughly north–south axis, while the other was destined to run from Davenport to a point on the Missouri River to be determined by the legislature of Iowa. Of particular note is a portion of the bill that required the railroad to complete the line promptly or risk the land being returned to the federal government, which would in essence be a death sentence to any further completion of the line. This particular fear was evidenced by a letter from the president of the M&M to the mayor of Davenport, published in the *Council Bluffs Nonpareil* on June 20, 1857. The railroad's president stated:

> *They believe that the interests of the company, of the State of Iowa, and of the city of Davenport especially, are deeply involved in the prompt execution of the work. They are already engaged in extensive operations....It is also a matter of good faith to Congress and the State to complete the line from Iowa City to Council Bluffs as speedily as possible.*

While the Rock Island and Chicago Railroad had made its way to the Illinois and Iowa border and the M&M was finding its feet, the struggle between water and rail transport continued to escalate. One focus point of the strife between the two systems played out in the opposing efforts of Chicago and St. Louis when it came to rail transport. St. Louis had benefited greatly from canal traffic and the trade that ran north–south along the Mississippi River. Meanwhile, the ever-expanding web of railroads emanating from Chicago was a boon to the economy there. In the 1850s, the two equally supported opposing views of how the transportation system of the new states would look. One such instance involved the building of a rail bridge to connect the Rock Island and Chicago to the M&M at Davenport, Iowa.

This conflict between the river commerce interests and railroads came to a head in 1862 during a court case over a bridge built jointly by the M&M and Rock Island and Chicago, in which James Ward sued the Mississippi and Missouri Railroad over what he saw as an illegal hazard to navigation across the river, claiming steamboats were entitled to the full riverbed. The lawsuit eventually reached the district court, which initially declared that the bridge was indeed in violation and should be abated. However, on further appeal, the case reached the Supreme Court in 1862. The court, acting in its unique ability to reverse lower court decisions, declared the bridge to be legal and allowed it to remain in place and, in doing so, provided the first legal victory to the railroad barons.

This declaration, while directly a victory for the M&M and the Rock Island and Chicago Railroads, was also an indirect victory for the rail industry as a whole. The argument between rail travel and canal or river travel was beginning to fall firmly on the side of rail travel. The difficulty in planning canal routes, in addition to the efficiency of railroads, was beginning to show that canals were slowly falling out of favor, driving more and more traffic to the railroads. The last major canal project, the Wabash and Erie Canal, reached its peak length in 1853 at 460 miles, making it the longest in the nation at the time. However, by 1860, the southern portions of the canal had fallen into disuse. The further development of the rail network, however, continued apace after 1853, with only a brief respite for the Civil War.

Shortly after the conclusion of the Civil War, the M&M was consolidated into the Rock Island and Chicago in August 1866. Upon the consolidation, the railroad took on the identity that would lead it through the rest of its life: Chicago, Rock Island and Pacific Railroad (CRI&P), alternatively known as the Rock Island Railroad or simply The Rock. It took the newly consolidated railroad another three years for it to reach the Missouri River in May 1869, nearly seventeen years after the railroad set out westward to reach the opposite border of Iowa.

The fourth Granger Railroad—the Chicago, Burlington and Quincy—found its foundations in 1849. An act to incorporate the Aurora Branch Railroad was passed through the Illinois legislature in February 1849. The original purpose for the Aurora Railroad Company was to be a branch line off the Galena and Chicago Union (G&CU) road to connect Aurora,

Illinois, to the G&CU Railroad using portions of the G&CU via trackage rights. By September 1850, despite delays from such events as unearthing mastodon tusks, the Aurora Branch had reached its namesake town, and plans were already in place to extend the line to the southwest to connect with the area of La Salle. The railroad was successful nearly immediately, with reports of strong profits on the back of lumber and pork transport reported in the *Illinois State Register* as early as December 1850.

It took another two years for the Illinois legislature to amend the charter, but in June 1852, the Aurora Branch received approval to extend their line to Mendota, Illinois, just north of La Salle, and officially change the name of the railroad to the Chicago and Aurora Railroad.

Only two years later, the Chicago and Aurora again received legislative approval to expand their line, this time to the city of Chicago itself, through the town of Naperville. It was through this same act that the railroad received its third name change in the five years since it was first created, the Chicago and Southwestern Railroad. The legislature further gave the railroad approval to consolidate with other railroads in the area, including the Northern Cross Railroad. The need for this extended line was an omen for things to come in the world of the Granger Railroads, as onerous fees were being exacted by the G&CU railroad for trackage rights into Chicago. However, the Chicago and Southwestern lasted only a year.

Nevertheless, the railroad continued to grow. In 1855, the Central Military Tract Railroad consolidated into the Chicago and Southwestern and became the Chicago, Burlington and Quincy (CB&Q), the name it would bear for much of the rest of its history until its final consolidation much later in the twentieth century. By 1861, another consolidation consumed the road from Yates City to St. David, Illinois, laid by the Jacksonville and Savannah Railroad Company. In 1864, in the throes of the Civil War, the CB&Q also acquired the system that began as the Peoria and Oquawka Railroad, and only a year later, it swallowed up the Northern Cross as well.

By the middle of the 1860s, the Granger Railroads had begun to reach their final form. By this point, the vast majority of the involvement of the state and federal governments was through the creation of railroad charters in the state legislatures and the issuance of land grants to states, which then doled them out to the various railroads. Beginning in 1850, the United States gave away millions of acres to corporations for railroad rights-of-way but also for helping the railroads to fund their endeavors through private land sales. Before Congress broke with tradition in 1862 and gave land directly to the Union Pacific, land grants were made to states directly, which then retained the ability to re-grant the land to whichever railroad they saw fit. It is estimated that in that time, more than seventy railroads were granted about 130.4 million acres from the federal government, an area slightly smaller than the state of Texas. Additionally, some states granted further lands to railroads when needed. The value of these lands is a question that has been debated for years; however, what is not debatable is that these land grants were a significant boon to the railroads and were also incredibly significant in their size. Generally speaking, the federal government did attempt to safeguard their grants by including deadlines for finishing roads and also provisions for fixing the rate of carriage for government freight. However, aside from these grants, very little was done by the United States to regulate the fledgling industry.

For much of the nineteenth century, the United States adopted what would later be called laissez-faire economics, a system where the federal government attempted to intervene as little as possible in the industries of the national economy. The Constitution did allow for economic regulation, so long as it was between states or a foreign power, under the "commerce clause" of Article 1. In 1824, the Supreme Court did show that the courts were willing to extend the commerce clause to both inter- and intrastate transportation industries in the case of *Gibbons v. Ogden*. Yet, as of the beginning of the Civil War, the federal government had yet to make any moves to regulate rail despite having the legal authority to do so.

It would fall then to the states to rein in the growing behemoth that had become the railroads of the 1860s. One such instance of state control was seen in Wisconsin, where the state legislature forbade a potential merger between the CNW and the Milwaukee and Prairie du Chien or the Milwaukee and St Paul. In an article from April 1867 in the *Semi-Weekly Wisconsin*, it is clear that railroad monopolies were already a concern for those living in the Granger states.

However, first, the Granger states needed to navigate a much stronger emergency, the Civil War. Much has been written about the relative advantage that the Union held over the Confederacy in terms of railroad mileage and industrial capacity, which is beyond the scope of this history. However, it is worth discussing the effect that the Civil War had on the rail industry in what could still be considered its early years of development.

The other major unintended legislative victory for the railroads in this early phase of their development, especially for the Granger Railroads, was the 1862 Homestead Act. The act, passed during the early years of the Civil War, stated that any citizen or intended citizen who had never waged war against the United States—an important caveat in 1862—could receive 160 acres provided they lived on and developed the land for five years with no charge, save for a registration fee or even a reduced six-month residency term for $1.25 per acre. As the Civil War drew to a close, to help provide for veterans, the bill was amended to allow veterans to deduct their service time from the residency requirements. In all, nearly 500 million acres of land were dispersed. While the efficacy of the act has come into question regarding its stated goal of creating plots for small farmers, some 80 million acres are estimated to have been granted to farmers in the West.

Land claims within the Homestead Act have widely been framed as fraudulent, and in some states, such as Iowa, previous land grabs and speculation, as well as railroad land grants, limited the amount of federal land available to private individuals. That being said, the Homestead

Family traveling west to their homestead. *United States National Archives.*

Act was especially important to the young state of Minnesota. During the initial wave of land claims in the 1860s, Minnesota saw the greatest amount of land claims out of the four Granger states. Land claims peaked in 1865, with nearly 4,000 claims amounting to 530,000 acres of land. By comparison, the peak of land claims in Iowa would not be until 1872, when a total of 264,000 acres were claimed, or Wisconsin's peak in 1863, when a total of 164,000 acres were claimed. Illinois, having been a state for the longest time, saw very little land left to claim under the act, and growth as a result of the 1862 act was negligible.

The population growth of the Granger states of Wisconsin, Iowa, Illinois and Minnesota during the height of the Homestead Act was staggering. According to the 1860 census, the total of these four states' population was a total of 3.33 million residents. However, by 1870, that number had nearly doubled to a staggering 5.23 million. Population statistics during this period alone cannot show the tremendous value that agriculture had within the region. Of the 1.9 million residents who flooded to the Midwest during that time, many chose to attempt to make their living farming the fertile lands in the Midwest.

Historic census data makes it difficult to get a clear picture of the workforce, but according to the best data available—the aforementioned census data from 1860 and 1870—we can get an effective picture of what the agricultural sector meant to these states. In 1860, there were 468,583 declared farmers or farm laborers in the four states of Wisconsin, Illinois, Iowa and Minnesota. Taken as a whole, these agricultural workers made up nearly 54 percent of the declared workforce. By 1870, the method of declaring occupations had changed, but the total number of "agricultural" workers in the four states was 821,518, with the proportion of the total population still standing around 54 percent. The states of Iowa and Minnesota stand out among the others as having farm populations that more than doubled in the ten-year period between the 1860 and 1870 census.

The Civil War has long been regarded as a "Railroad War," and much has been written regarding the relative strengths the Union possessed when it comes to railroad infrastructure. These discussions are, as mentioned earlier, largely outside of the scope of this discussion, other than to say that the railroads of the Union states prospered, while the infrastructure grew significantly less during the years of the war. As the Civil War came to a close and manifest destiny continued its march toward the west, the Granger Roads stood poised to reap the benefits of an economy and population growing by leaps and bounds. However, the people of the Midwest soon learned that economic progress left unchecked can often have consequences that outweigh its benefits. A conflict was brewing: this time, instead of force of arms, the people of the Midwest used their political influence not to fight their fellow countrymen but the corporations controlling the growing transportation system.

2

THE CIVIL WAR AND POSTWAR PERIOD

AGRICULTURE AND RAIL MONOPOLIES

The Civil War began in April 1861 with the shelling of Fort Sumter in South Carolina. Decades of tension regarding the expansion of slavery had boiled over into a cataclysmic conflict between the Confederate States of America mainly situated south of the Mason–Dixon line, and the remaining United States mostly in the North, often referred to as simply the Union. Geographically and ideologically split, the two sides spilled the blood of relatives and former countrymen for four years before the guns fell silent. The conflict proved to be bloody, surpassing even World War II in terms of American lives lost.

The Civil War was a transformative period in U.S. history for numerous reasons, including but not limited to, the end of slavery, the creation of the Fourteenth Amendment to guarantee equal protection to all Americans and a rapid increase in medical technology, as well as new industrial techniques, which all resulted from this dark period. The period was enormously consequential for the rail industry and the Midwest as well.

Grain prices had been rising in the years before the Civil War in the Midwest. Iowa in particular saw a windfall harvest in 1860. According to the *North Iowa Times*, in the summer of 1860, wheat prices at McGregor, Iowa, were quoted at $0.88 to $0.92 per bushel. Furthermore, the harvest was expected to "very far exceed the anticipations of the most sanguine." By September, the paper was reporting that "prices are to rule higher than they have for the last 20 years." Specifically, the paper mentioned that by July of the previous year, around one million bushels had been transported, but the 1860 harvest was expected to surpass three million bushels. Like many other riverfront cities, McGregor was an economically important city to Iowa. McGregor was a connection point to the CM&SP (Milwaukee Road), providing one of the more convenient points for farmers in northeastern Iowa to have their grain shipped to the markets of the East Coast.

While inflation was to blame for some of the cost increases during the Civil War, the price of grain well outpaced the inflationary state of the Union economy. In 1863, the *North Iowa Times* again reported on the price of wheat, this time in February, giving the price to be around $1.12 per bushel locally or $1.27 in the Milwaukee market. This $0.15 price differential between the frontier towns and the major commercial centers of the Midwest was significant, but more significant was the difference in price between Chicago or Milwaukee and the East Coast markets. According to a February issue of the *Buffalo Commercial*, the price of Milwaukee wheat in the New York market was trading around $1.62, a whole $0.35 more than the price quoted at Milwaukee for the same time.

Meanwhile, the railroads were charging significant amounts of money to transport wheat by rail. In September 1861, the *North Iowa Times* reported that the M&PdC was forced to drop their wheat rates from $0.14 per bushel to $0.10 per bushel due to competition from steamboats along with the La Crosse and Milwaukee road.

Much of the farming being done in the North was increasingly mechanized during this time as well. John Deere invented the first steel-bladed plow in 1837, making farming significantly easier in the thick fertile soils of the upper Midwest. Cyrus McCormick patented the first mechanical reaper in 1834, and soon a flood of new horse-powered farm implements found their way to market in order to ease the burden on farmers and improve output. In 1863, an advertisement in the *Centralia Sentinel* promoted automated corn planters, mechanical harvesters, mowers and reapers, threshing machines, sugarcane mills, evaporators, horse rakes, mowers and straw cutters.

Much of this machinery was sent North, especially to the farms of the Midwest, where labor was scarce. The Southern states with their prewar reliance on enslaved labor did not readily adopt labor-saving devices, with the noted exception of the cotton gin. This led to a great discrepancy in food crop production between the Union and Confederacy, which played

Advertisement for McCormick Reaper. *Wisconsin Historic Society*.

out through the war and drove Northern farmers to produce as much as they could. The increased demand for grain allowed the farmers to absorb the ever-increasing freight rates that railroads often charged for their products.

Farmers benefited from a wartime economy in which grain was a prominent commodity. The old quote "An army marches on its stomach," frequently attributed to Napoleon, was just as true of the Union army as it was for Napoleon's fateful march into Russia. According to the U.S. Army War College, a Union soldier received around one pound of bread and three-quarters to a pound of meat depending on the variety per day. By 1863, the ranks of the Union army had risen to some 600,000 men, meaning the demand for grain products from the new farms of the Midwest was at an all-time high, and farmers were more than happy to produce. Beyond the human cost of food, the vast number of animals that the army employed required an equally vast amount of food and forage to support them. In the winter of 1861–62, the army estimated in a study titled *Quartermaster Support of the Army; a History of the Corps, 1775–1939* that the Army of the Potomac alone required four hundred tons of forage for their animal.

Another factor driving the farming economy of the Civil War was a significant lack of manpower. As more and more farmers left to fight

Civil War Supply Depot with rail connections in City Point, Virginia. *Library of Congress.*

and die on the battlefields, mechanization and labor-saving became paramount. This drive for production through efficiency drove up yields. There was also a concurrent need in Europe for increased grain imports. By 1860, Britain could produce only around three-fourths of its needed wheat and began to look to the United States and mainland Europe to help bridge the gap. At the height of imports in 1862, Great Britain imported nearly five million quarters, equivalent to around forty million bushels, of grain to help to feel the island's population. The loss of cotton sales for the Southern states, combined with the increase in grain sales from the Union, further laid bare the economic disparity between the two belligerents.

During the Civil War, railroads experienced a sudden boom in shipping. Not only was grain being produced in record amounts and shipped east, but the army was also quick to utilize the emerging national network of railroads to ship men and material to the front. In the early days of the war, there was a significant amount of profiteering done by the railroads, especially in the West. In the previously mentioned quartermaster study, it was determined that in St. Louis in particular, rates were not being competitively sought, and as a result, railroads were competing for highly profitable passenger rates. Furthermore, some railroads were overcharging the army when compared with private freight, in some cases netting as much as $20,000 over and above what they would have gotten with a fair quote.

Despite the profiteering that was alleged, the Union railroad system did face some challenges during this time as well. Much of the Northern system, in contrast to the modern rail system, had no set gauge. This meant that freight moving from one road to the next might necessitate a change from one car to another wherever two roads met with different gauges. This difficulty was noted in the quartermaster's report through an anecdote: "Carrying out orders from Thomas A. Scott, he altered within 11 days the gauge of the tracks of the Louisville and Frankfort and the Lexington and Frankfort Railroads (some 95 miles in all) from 4 feet 8.5 inches to 5 feet. Cars and engines were made to conform. As a result, supplies could be loaded at Covington, Ky., and run through to the Army south of Nashville without transfer of freight at Louisville."

Nevertheless, the North experienced a vast advantage in rail logistics, which played a significant role in both battlefield tactics as well as overall logistical planning. The North held a more than 2:1 advantage in rail miles, as well as a more than 3:1 population advantage. Not only could the Union field more men, but they could also get those men more quickly to the front and make sure that their supplies could be more readily produced and reach the front in a quick and efficient manner.

By January 1862, the army had straightened out many of the issues regarding pricing and had secured rates that were below published private freight rates across the rail system. The rail system in the West experienced a monopoly during this time as well. The Mississippi River had been closed to traffic, as the natural terminus of the river existed in New Orleans, Louisiana, which as of January 1861 had joined the Confederate States. It would not be until 1863, after the fall of Vicksburg, that the river reopened to commercial traffic. However, as noted by Emerson D. Fite in a 1906 article titled "The Agricultural Development of the West During the Civil War" in *The Quarterly Journal of Economics*, "The opening of the river in 1863 had no appreciable effect in starting traffic again southward, because marauders on both banks continued to make the route unsafe, and because the westerners had come to appreciate the speed and directness of the northern route."

Even among the Union, the free states of the Midwest held firm as the leader in rail mileage. The first age of rail consolidation also meant that the Granger railroads, yet to take on this monicker, whether in their final form or not by the outset of the war, were in a position to have a direct outcome on the war and to profit from it. With all of the economic activity the war brought, it is no surprise that the railroads were able to recover from the panic of 1857. However, one of the most momentous undertakings in the history of rail travel in the United States had yet to emerge from the Civil War.

IOWA
ILLINOIS
ARKANSAS
LAKE MICHIGAN
LAKE ERIE
HURON
DETROIT AND MILWAUKEE RAIL-ROAD
GEORGIA RAIL ROAD
MEMPHIS AND CHARLESTON
NASHVILLE
CLEVELAND
ATLANTA
MOBILE
SELMA
OPELIKA
HELENA
CONWAY
GRAND GULF
NATCHEZ
LAKE PONTCHARTRAIN

American Railroads Map of the Civil War. *David Rumsey Map Archive.*

Plans for a railroad that would connect the two coasts of the United States began nearly concurrently with the acquisition of the territories on the Pacific coast. In 1845, Asa Whitney petitioned Congress for a land grant from Lake Michigan to the Pacific coast crossing the Rocky Mountains and heading northwest to the Oregon Territory. This brought about opposition from Illinois in the way of Stephen A. Douglas, who, according to the *Washington Union* newspaper, published a letter advocating for a route that would emanate from Chicago connecting with Council Bluffs and onto San Francisco. Interestingly, this push from Whitney came before the final territorial borders were negotiated with Great Britain in 1846, demonstrating the fervor with which many Americans of the age were treating the concept of manifest destiny and the push to the West.

In 1849, Whitney published a pamphlet to garner attention for his desire to build a road to the west, still advocating the route that connected through Wisconsin. Whitney's argument in *A Project for Railroad to the Pacific* possessed considerable foresight into his plan, predicting the later sectional conflict over the route as well as Congress's frugality in helping to fund the road. Whitney's plan rested on a significant land grant of thirty miles along either side of the proposed route. In reality, this land was to be sold to Whitney, although he suggested a rate of ten cents per acre, which he would then turn around and resell to use as a means to pay workers and generate settlement along the route. This would provide funding for the road as well as the right-of-way, yet he also understood the rapid settling of the Midwest was putting this plan at risk of failing before it could start.

Nevertheless, Whitney did not see his road completed, let alone started. It was another four years before the federal government took any actions related to a transcontinental railroad. In March 1853, Congress passed An Act Making Appropriations for the Support of the Army for the Year Ending Fourteenth of June, One Thousand Eight Hundred and Fifty-Four, and nestled into section 10 of the aforementioned bill was an appropriation of $150,000 for the Army Corps of Topographical Engineers to survey a route from the Mississippi River to the West Coast. This appropriation stands with the course of federal support for rail in the first half of the nineteenth century; rather than directly subsidizing or regulating the roads, the federal government was content to assist with survey and land grants across the vast and untamed interior of federal lands.

At the conclusion of the survey, led by Secretary of War and future Confederate President Jefferson Davis, sectional infighting ensued over

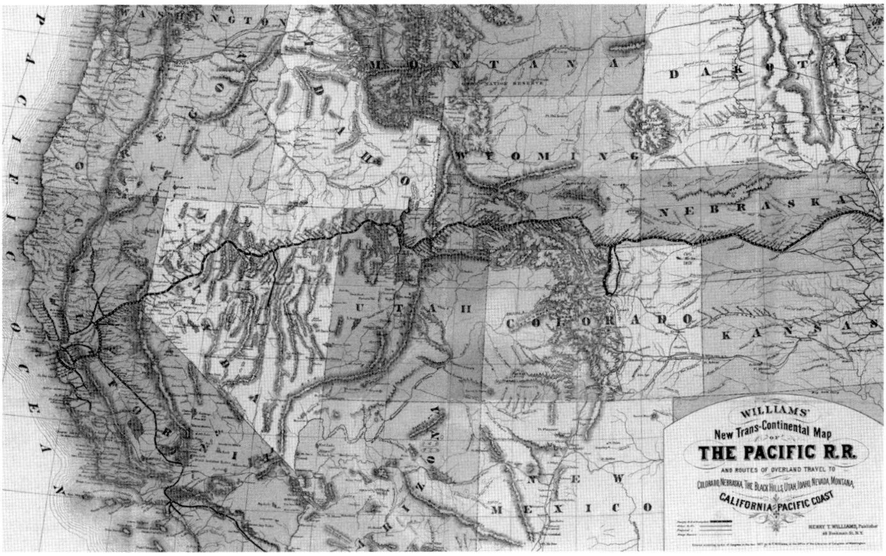

Proposed Transcontinental Pacific Railroad Map. *Library of Congress.*

whether the line should favor a more southerly route or northerly route, mirroring the state of national politics in the 1850s. It was nine more years before Congress took the next steps toward the completion of a railroad to connect the coasts. On July 1, 1862, Congress passed An Act to Aid in the Construction of a Railroad and Telegraph Line from the Missouri River to the Pacific Ocean, and to Secure the Government the Use of the Same for Postal, Military, and Other Purposes, more commonly known as the Pacific Railroad Act. This act incorporated a company known as the Union Pacific Railroad Company. The railroad was to be funded by the sale of 100,000 shares of stock, sold at a price of $1,000 each. The Union Pacific was also granted an extensive land grant of two hundred feet to either side of the route from which the railroad was given the right to use whatever natural resources were needed to build the railroad or to build infrastructure to support the railroad, with additional alternating sections of land to be granted to help support the railroad.

On July 10, 1865, the Union Pacific laid its first tracks, and by 1869, the Union and Central Pacific railroads met at Promontory Summit in Utah, completing the route from Omaha to Sacramento. However, the full connection to the East was not yet complete; it would not be until 1872, when a bridge connected Omaha to Council Bluffs on March 14, and the *Sioux City Journal* reported that the bridge spanning the Missouri River was open for business. This finally connected the Union Pacific to rails that allowed a direct route across the entire nation. This also allowed the midwestern roads, especially those with connections to Council Bluffs such as the Rock Island Railroad, to access the new West Coast markets as well.

When the dust finally settled on the Civil War, the U.S. economy emerged stronger than before, especially in the North, where industrial production during the war had helped to further encourage development. Settlement of the West was also encouraged by the wartime Pacific Railroad Act and the Homestead Act, both of which were only accessible to citizens of Southern states after the end of the war. However, as this economic prosperity continued, the relative lack of federal regulation on business meant that as railroads and their influence grew, there were no guardrails to protect the population from the ill effects of the new corporations.

In 1865, according to *History of the Grange Movement* by James D. McCabe, railroads in the United States held 34,442 miles, an increase of nearly 4,000 miles from the outset of the war in 1861. Furthermore, McCabe noted that by 1872, the "western states" had a significant majority of the track miles in the United States, some 34,000 miles out of a total of 62,000. It was in this period of postwar expansion that the Granger Railroads came to the forefront.

In 1865, following its merger with the Galena Union Railroad, the CNW became one of the longest single railroad systems in the United States at a staggering 860 route miles when including leased track. This new network dwarfed the next nearest competitor, the Illinois Central, with its 706 miles. This era of railroad history is marked by consolidation, as illustrated in chapter 1. The railroads of the upper Midwest grew mostly out of acquisition rather than through organic expansion. Railroads quickly discovered that economies of scale led to much more efficient operation, and the days of small regional or statewide railroads came to a close. In their place came interstate corporations running near 1,000-mile networks crisscrossing multiple states.

Meanwhile, the Milwaukee Road continued its postwar expansion as well, reaching the lofty heights of the CNW's track mileage by 1868 when 825 miles of track were being utilized in route service across the midwestern states. In 1872, the railroad acquired the Chicago & St. Paul along with its trackage along the east coast of Minnesota, and in 1874, it completed its connection between Milwaukee and Chicago, changing its name to Chicago, Milwaukee and St. Paul.

Likewise, the Chicago, Burlington and Quincy was experiencing a surge as well in the waning years of the Civil War. The smallest of the Granger Railroads had under its control nearly four hundred miles of track. However, unlike the others, the CB&Q had the entirety of its tracks within one state, Illinois. In the late 1860s, the CB&Q inaugurated bridge-building projects that would give it connections to the Burlington and Missouri at Burlington, Iowa, as well as the Hannibal and St. Joseph Railroad in Missouri. Despite its small size, the CB&Q, or more appropriately its Hannibal and St. Joseph sister line, was the host of the first Railway Post Office car in 1862 by converting old luggage cars. While this initial experiment was short-lived, the CNW later inaugurated the first dedicated Railway Post Office cars, cementing mail service as a cornerstone of the growing railroad networks.

With the ever-expanding network of rails connecting disparate cities throughout what was still very much a frontier nation, the railroad and U.S. Postal Service made for a natural symbiosis in the latter part of the nineteenth century. Though the West Coast of the United States was largely settled, there were still large tracts of uninhabited wildland between the relatively populated Midwest and the growing West Coast cities.

Before regular rail mail service, the United States had used various means to move mail from its East to West Coast, the first attempt being a steamship passage from the East Coast to Panama, then overland to the Pacific before again being shipped by sea to the West Coast, a time-consuming and expensive proposition. The Overland Mail Company used stagecoaches to ferry mail between Missouri and California. Yet these methods made for mail delivery times measured in weeks rather than days.

Perhaps the best-known method for delivering mail prior to train service was the Pony Express. Created in 1860 to address the issue of delivering mail in less time, it was a relay system of horseback riders. Riders raced in 10-mile segments across the Wild West from St. Joseph Missouri to San Francisco. In all, a letter traveling the Pony Express route took ten days to make the 1,966-mile journey to San Francisco, a drastic reduction from steamship or stagecoach travel. The Pony Express, an idea ancient in its origins, represented the best option for communication across the nation for only one short year, until a telegraph line connected the western and eastern halves of the nation and the final spike in the Transcontinental Railroad was driven at Promontory Point in 1869, making even stagecoach trips obsolete.

The first records of the U.S. Postal Service using rail transport date back to 1832 in Pennsylvania; by 1835, about 1 percent of all U.S. Mail was being carried by rail. In 1865, when Union Pacific began operations, the Railway Mail Service was created to manage U.S. Mail across the rail networks of the growing nation, about five years after the first regular use of Railway Post Office cars to sort mail en route. At its peak, in the early twentieth century, the Railway Mail Service ran on nearly ten thousand trains, a far cry from the humble beginnings in St. Joseph, Missouri. This new marriage of government financial might and technology led to a metaphorical shrinking of the nation, cutting communication times in half. It also provided a steady stream of income to the fledgling railroads, just now emerging from the boom-and-bust cycle that characterized much of the first half of the nineteenth century.

It was only in the late 1860s and '70s that many of the Midwest railroads could conceivably make good on the "Pacific" portions of their company names. Manifest destiny was a very real and powerful force working within the United States in the late nineteenth century. While the romantic vision of Conestoga wagons and the Oregon Trail captured the imagination, it was the railroads that would satisfy the thirst for westward expansion after the Civil War. This rapid expansion created a demand for raw materials, which the industrialized eastern states were happy to supply.

The United States had, by the outbreak of the war, already experienced rapid economic growth. Between 1800 and 1860, the GDP per capita had nearly doubled, and the prospects after the war were just as positive. To take another perspective, the National Bureau of Economic Research published GNP, or gross national product, figures from the decade preceding and following the Civil War. According to their report, the GNP, in 1860 dollars, for the decade before the Civil War, stood at $3.3 billion, while the decade following the Civil War, stood at $6.4 billion. This rapid growth made many people within the United States very wealthy, ushering in the Gilded Age, known for its opulent shows of wealth by the growing upper class, juxtaposed by the abject poverty felt by the lower working class. While this period eventually gave way to the Progressive Era, fixing many of the social ills created during the Gilded Age, one group that was ready for immediate action was farmers.

Throughout the country's history, farmers have been cited as the backbone of the American economy and, in some cases, democracy. From the pioneers who set off through the Cumberland Gap to the homesteaders who settled the West, these farmers fed the ever-growing East while barely eking out a living on the plains. In the years following the Civil War, several complaints among farmers grew into a crescendo, which led to one of the more impressive fringe political movements to sweep the country.

Farmers' complaints throughout history have often gone back to economics, and the complaints of farmers in the post–Civil War era were no different. Farmers complained that prices were falling, owing in large part to the overproduction driven by the wartime economy. Further, they complained that their dwindling profits were being eaten by monopolistic railroads and grain elevator operators who were charging discriminatory prices to farmers, the very groups who had often so vigorously supported their construction. Lastly, farmers felt unfairly treated by the banks, which they claimed were giving predatory loans with rates higher than they ought to for land and materials. While there have been many attempts to verify or discredit these claims throughout the years, at the time, these farmers felt that their situation was dire enough to warrant banding together to protect their way of life and their economic freedom.

The agricultural community had enough. Led by a pioneering Minnesotan named Oliver Kelly, an organization rose out of the ashes of the Civil War to lead the fight for farmers' grievances. Founded as a fraternal organization along similar lines to the Masonic Order, the National Grange of the Order of the Patrons of Husbandry became one of the most prominent social organizations of the late nineteenth century, wielding enormous social and political power, not only in the Midwest but throughout the nation as well. Its name was eventually grafted onto the railroads that it fought against and has become a symbol of grassroots organization and democratic engagement, yet it has also become a cautionary tale of the power of a tyrannical majority that the founding fathers of the United States once cautioned against.

The National Grange of the Order of the Patrons of Husbandry, more popularly called simply the Grange, was founded officially in late 1868 in Washington, D.C. Within a few short years, Grange halls had begun to pop up all across the nation and, most importantly for the railroads, in the midwestern states. In Kelly's home state of Minnesota, forty chapters had opened up by 1870 alone. Within five years, nearly one million farmers throughout the nation were counted among the rolls of the Grange, scattered amongst some nine thousand chapters.

The speed with which the organization grew spoke to the concern that farmers had with their livelihoods during this period in history. According to James Steward of Reed College, agricultural prices during the first three years of the 1870s showed a steady decline from year to year, due in part to ecological effects of drought but also due to overproduction. According to the United States Department of Agriculture, the price of U.S. corn was listed as $0.52 per bushel and fell to an alarming $0.38 by 1872, with a simultaneous increase of over 100 million bushels

Gifts of the Granger poster advertising the National Grange, 1873. *Library of Congress.*

nationwide. Similarly, in December 1870, the price of pork was reported in the *Morning Democrat* of Davenport, Iowa, as $18.25 on the Chicago Market; however, it had fallen to $13.30 by December of the following year. The same story was being played out across the nation's farming center, and farmers were feeling the squeeze. However, it seemed as if one industry, once hailed as the savior of the midwestern farmer, was doing very well at the same time the farmers were struggling: the railroads.

Gauging the success or lack thereof of a company can be a complicated task. Increased earnings do not always equate to a healthier business, and increased costs or a year or two in the red don't always indicate a company that is failing. That being said, we can gain some insight into the financial and physical state of these railroads through their annual reports, which give stockholders some idea of the railroad's year-to-year activities.

If we look at the Chicago and Northwestern in May 1873, just months before the great panic of 1873, the CNW gave the following update. Their new rail laid equated to 145.4 miles, bringing total operating mileage up to 1459.5 miles. Yet it is the earnings and expenses report of the CNW that really brought the farmers' concerns into focus. The gross earnings for 1873 were listed as $12,736,606.75, with operating expenses of $8,178,236.71, for a total net revenue of around $4.5 million, equivalent to around $114.6 million in 2023. Among the listed sources of revenue, freight revenue was valued at over $8.6 million, more than two-thirds of the total, at the same time farmers were experiencing year-on-year price drops.

Meanwhile, according to their annual reports, the Chicago, Burlington and Quincy were, for the year 1874, posting net earnings of $5,131,805.13. Freight made up around $8.45 million of the gross income total of $11.64 million. While the CB&Q was earning significantly less than the CNW, when the trackage of the CB&Q is taken into account, 787 miles, the CB&Q was keeping up with the CNW on a revenue-per-mile basis. The story is the same for the other major midwestern roads: while the farmers were failing to gain ground and, in many cases, falling further into debt, the railroads were posting ever higher profits.

Farmers were becoming increasingly discontent with their economic situation, especially with the railroads they once saw as saviors. With little to no economic strength to change the situation, they, with their strength in numbers through the Grange, turned to the only place they could, politics. Postwar American politics were anything but simple. The years of Reconstruction were still well in motion during the rise of the farmers' rights movement, and the wounds from the Civil War were far from healed. However, with no alternative, the farmers chose to test the waters and put into motion one of the most successful grassroots advocacy movements in the nation.

General Ulysses S. Grant. *Library of Congress.*

In 1873, Congress was a far cry from anything that the farmers had seen in much of their lives. The 1870 census had been the first in the nation to incorporate African Americans into the count fully, and the resultant reapportionment meant that the political landscape of the United States had been significantly altered. New coalitions were being created, and a new sense of optimism in the political process was empowering citizens around the nation to take on the issues they once saw as impossible obstacles.

3

THE FIRST GRANGER LAWS AND THE PANIC OF 1873

The Granger movement, while in name and practice a national movement, found its greatest success in what were then known as the "western states" or, as we know it in the twenty-first century, the Midwest. According to a contemporary work chronicling the rise of, and argument for, the National Grange called *History of the Grange Movement* by James McCabe, the National Brotherhood of the Grange had nearly 10,000 local chapters called subordinate Granges. Of these "sub-granges," Iowa alone had 1,845 chapters, Illinois had another 821, Minnesota had 405 and Wisconsin was home to 289.

When put together, these states boasted nearly a third of all the chapters in the United States. The growth of the Grange movement was picking up steam. In 1872, across the entire nation, the Grange movement added 1,053 subordinate granges, while in 1873, they added 8,672 chapters, an 823 percent increase. In 1873, the membership was estimated at over 751,000 individuals, a staggering amount considering the entire U.S. population in 1870 was estimated at just over 38,000,000, meaning that very nearly 2 percent of the entire population of the United States was a member. If the membership numbers are broken down even further, there is a substantial rise in sub-Grange additions in the last four months of 1873, during the financial crisis known as the Panic of 1873, one of the worst economic disasters to befall the nation until the dark days of the late 1920s and 1930s.

However, we must first understand why, in particular, the states of the upper-Midwest were so keen to join a farmers' movement and what this movement's goals and aspirations were that made it so appealing. As discussed in the previous chapter, the movement had been around for some time by the events of the Panic of 1873. By the late 1860s and early 1870s, the Grange was making a name for itself by taking on what it saw as the monopolistic actions of the railroads, which members saw as directly threatening western farmers. As has already been made clear in previous chapters, the farmers initially saw the railroads as a positive economic force in their lives, even going so far as to fund them through bonds in many cases. Access to eastern markets, especially in the days of high prices and near limitless demand during the Civil War, gave the Midwest its reputation as the breadbasket of the nation and gave many farmers a very comfortable living.

However, in the days of flat or even falling crop prices following the conclusion of the war, farmers were beginning to feel the pinch of low demand met with overproduction. What's more, they began to feel that the railroads, once seen as their savior, were now actively working to wring as much money as they could from the very farmers that had once supported and even funded their creation. In his book, McCabe quoted an Iowa farmer as saying:

> *The railroads of this state discriminate unjustly against the farmers in the transportation of crops; that is, give other men advantages which they deny to the farmers.*

The farmer went on to explain that whenever crops needed to be sent east, farmers would ship whatever surplus crops were not needed in local markets to the east. Often buying agents would purchase entire harvests and then contract the railroads to ship at a lower bulk rate. However, it seems, according to the farmer interviewed, that whenever the farmers banded together to cut out the middleman, the rates they received were significantly higher and often such that they received next to nothing for the crop by the time it reached the eastern market.

It can be easy to understand then why farmers, especially in states so dependent on agriculture as those in the Midwest, could see an organization like the Grange as a force for good in their lives. The Grange was avowedly apolitical and without a religious slant. That is to say, they declined to take any sides both politically and religiously, something that would've been a relief to a nation wracked by political division in the days of Reconstruction. In an 1870 article in the *Southern Argus*, the general deputy of the order,

C.C. Hutchinson, was quoted as saying, "The Patrons of Husbandry is in no sense a political organization….Religious or political questions will not be tolerated as subjects of discussion in the work of the Order." This would've been especially appealing to the diverse group of settlers from across Europe and the United States that had settled across the region in the latter half of the nineteenth century.

Furthermore, the Grange was set up with farmers and their personal wealth in mind. In the same article, Hutchinson asserted, "Our order is founded on the axiom that the products of the soil comprise the basis of all wealth, and to increase these products is our aim." The Grange would have found no difficulty in recruiting farmers in the late 1860s and early 1870s with the rhetoric of more wealth and no discrimination. The order was also in accord with the farmers in one other regard during this time: cutting out the profiteering middlemen who seemed to be preying on the farmers at each turn. Hutchinson went on, "The patrons of husbandry wish to bring the producer and the consumer into more immediate relations…. That society supports too many drones has come to be an axiom, and how to get rid of them is no new problem."

As with many large fraternal organizations that allegedly wield outsized power, however, the patrons were also operating a closed society, one that kept its inner workings a secret. However, Hutchinson had a rather simple explanation for this secrecy: "to promote efficiency, extension and unity, and to establish among its members confidence, harmony, and security." As it was then, by the dawn of the 1870s, the Patrons of Husbandry were a growing organization full of farmers wishing to find a way to regain the upper hand in the economic struggle that had befallen them in the wake of the Civil War, just when the farmers would need the help the most. Yet even before the Panic of 1873, the Grange made the first move in the David and Goliath duel against the captains of industry running the railroads.

In early 1871, a year after a new constitution was established in Illinois, the state's General Assembly passed a series of laws that hoped to rein in the railroads and placed them under the watchful eye of the state railroad commission. These laws would be the first so-called Granger Laws established in the midwestern farming states as the pressure from the National Grange pushed legislators into action.

While passenger rates were regulated by Illinois in the 1870s, the laws regulating freight rates and more specifically rate discrimination struck right at the root of the issues the Grange hoped to address. Hopes were not high, according to some newspaper accounts in the spring of 1870, that

Bird's-eye view of the Chicago Stock Yards, 1878. *Library of Congress.*

any progress would indeed be made. In the *Rock Island Argus* on March 23, 1871, an article detailing actions in the General Assembly read, "It is true that the people who are being ground down by these railroad corporations are crying for legislation, but the radical legislature will adjourn and not one item of relief will they have received." Despite this outlook, only a month later, the General Assembly passed the first laws designed specifically to limit the power of the railroads to discriminate in their rates.

When passed, the laws ushered in a new age in Illinois: no longer were the railroads able to freely set rates, as had been the case since their incorporation, but now strict rules governed both passenger and freight rates or tariffs as they were referred to at the time. Among the various provisions included were prohibitions against local freight versus through freight discrimination, laws regarding accurate scales at grain elevators and prohibitions against discriminatory rates between large- and small-scale shippers, as well as a prohibition against raising rates to cover costs incurred from the new laws, essentially locking in rates at their 1870 levels. These laws also came with strict penalties, such as a fine of $1,000 or even the loss of the railroad's charter to operate within Illinois. To enforce these new laws, the state created a railroad commission to oversee the operations of the various companies and to ensure their accurate reporting.

At least initially, reports pointed to an amicable relationship between the railroads and the commission. In the *Pantograph*, a Bloomington, Illinois newspaper, in July 1871 it was reported that "the commissioners appear to have established the best relationship between themselves and the railroad companies." In August, the *Nashville Journal* reported positively on the appointment of an ex-governor to the Railroad

Commission, further showing the public approval of both the legislation and the commission itself.

Elsewhere in the Midwest, work was well underway toward reining in the various railroads of the other states. In June 1871, the Republican Party of the state of Iowa met for its annual convention. Among their resolutions was a call for restrictive railroad legislation. Ultimately, change in Iowa was still a few years off, despite the strong presence of the Grange within the state. Meanwhile, in Minnesota, calls were made early in the year; according to the *Star Tribune*, a special committee of the Minnesota Senate called for the appointment of a railroad commissioner to look into legislation to regulate rails within the state.

In March 1871, the state passed a law bringing its own railroad commission into being. The office, in multiple forms over the years, was primarily tasked with obtaining information for the state legislature as to the adherence of the railroads within the state to their regulations, their financial status and their physical maintenance status. The commissioner, while independent as a part of the executive branch of the state government, was required to report to the legislature within the first week of each session about the various railroads within the state. We can glean from this setup that the legislature was not only concerned with the legal status of the railroads but also understood their valuable and, in many cases, essential economic placement within the state.

Minnesota eventually followed in the regulatory footsteps of Illinois and passed laws forbidding rate discrimination, as well as requiring much more detailed information to rein in the excesses of the railroads, but this law would not come until an expansion of the railroad commissioner into a three-member commission in 1885. The Granger railroads were slowly being brought to heel by the very farmers they had been created for and, in many cases, by. However, it was an event in 1873 that would further drive the farmers into the arms of the Grange and their radical railroad reforms.

While the nation seemed to be recovering well from the dark days of the Civil War, it was also becoming much more connected with the global economy. The grain from the Midwest, now easily shipped to the coasts, was reaching European markets; cotton from the South supplied the British textile mills, and luxury products from Europe were arriving on the East Coast to be shipped inland by myriad new mail-order retailers. Yet as was often the case, much of this economic activity was sitting atop a shaky foundation. A combination of stock market scares in Vienna, Austria, and New York cascaded between Europe and North America, as an investment bubble, of which many railroads had been beneficiaries, began to pop. One of the most eventful failures was that of the Northern Pacific Railroad, meant to connect Lake Superior to the Pacific coast, when its main benefactor, Jay Cooke & Co., went bankrupt.

While the nation narrowly avoided the cascading bank failures that would characterize the Great Depression of the 1920s and 1930s, it did not escape an intense period of economic malaise. The New York Stock Exchange took drastic action, as reported by the *Kingston Daily Freeman*; just before noon, the president of the NYSE closed operations, deemed a master stroke by the paper's writers, before the panic could fully engulf the trading floor. However, the damage was done: many banks had already failed, and more were feared to fail shortly. Worst of all, many of the stocks and bonds most heavily affected were those of the railroads. Railroads had capitalized on the investment craze of the postwar era to finance construction or expansion, and with funding quickly drying up, times were going to be tough for the nation's economic lifeline.

Railroads began to feel the pinch and quickly hit back at those who had previously invested. In November 1873, the Kansas-Pacific Railroad, another midwestern railroad, needed to stop payment interest payments on its bonded debt. Even the titans of the rail industry were not immune

Wood engraving depicting the suspension of Jay Cooke & Co. at the New York Stock Exchange. *Northern Illinois University Archives.*

to the effects of the panic. In October 1873, the *Clinton Register* reported that Cornelius Vanderbilt's New York Central Railroad stock had fallen 7 percent in a mid-October aftershock to the market. The panic had now reached the most powerful of rail empires in the nation and was wreaking havoc on investors and businessmen alike, all to the detriment of the farmers whose livelihoods depended on the continued operations of the midwestern rail network. It was in the midst of this time of financial ruin and hardship for the rail industry that the next Granger state passed one of the most stringent and influential of the Granger Laws, Potter's Law.

In 1874, Wisconsin was home to, according to reports published in the *Wood County Reporter*, 167 Granges with some 6,414 members. The largest Grange in the state was in Evansville with nearly 150 members. In the same article, regarding the actions of various state Grange meetings, it is clear that the Grange in late 1873 and early 1874 was actively pursuing an agenda of economic regulation for the benefit of farmers. The article reported that in Michigan, the Grange was exploring railroad regulation. In Wisconsin, the Grange favored "combined actions" against any company that would not give wholesale rates to Grange agencies.

The power of the Grange movement in Wisconsin was further demonstrated by the elections of 1873, which created a government amenable to restrictive railroad legislation. The Granger movement had coalesced in the state of Wisconsin into a formidable political force, electing several offices throughout the state, most notably Governor William Robert Taylor. According to a profile from the *Iowa County Democrat* in December 1873, the governor-elect was a transplant to Wisconsin from the Northeast, a farmer and a prominent member of the Granger movement. Taylor was said to have advocated a break from the Democratic Party, creating a new party aimed at addressing some of the issues the Granger movement was most concerned about.

Passed on March 11, 1874, Wisconsin Chapter 273, more popularly known as the Potter Law, placed strict price controls on the state's railroads and created a commission to oversee the railroads and enforce the new laws. The law set out a complex series of railroad classifications, by which the commission determined how much could be charged per mile for passengers. The passenger classes were divided as Class A (the largest railroads in the state such as CNW and Milwaukee Road), Class B and Class C. Class A roads were the most strictly limited and could charge only \$0.03 per mile for passengers, while Class B and C were allowed \$0.035 and \$0.04 per mile, respectively. The freight rules were even more complex, divided into four general classes and seven more specific classes. Of particular note was Class D freight, which was all grain shipments.

Portrait of Wisconsin's Governor Taylor. *Wisconsin Historic Society*.

The railroads were already seeing the writing on the wall by early 1874. The *Grant County Herald* reported that John W. Crary, attorney for the Chicago, Milwaukee and St. Paul, petitioned the railroad committee for over two hours in February 1874, trying to explain how it was the farmers oppressing the railroads and not the other way around. In April 1874, the heads of the Milwaukee Road and Chicago and North Western met in Chicago to determine, according to the *Wisconsin State Journal*, "what actions it was advisable for them to take in regard to the new railroad, or Granger laws of Iowa, Minnesota, and Wisconsin."

However, the railroad efforts were to no avail, and by the time spring turned to summer, the railroad law was taking effect. In May 1874, it was reported that the presidents of the Chicago and North Western as well as the Chicago, Milwaukee and St. Paul had written letters, later published and reported by the *Dodgeville Chronicle* on May 8, 1874, stating they would not conform to the new rates. The rates were so low as to drive the railroads out of business, and the railroads intended to challenge the laws in court. A showdown was scheduled for June in the Wisconsin Supreme Court between Wisconsin Attorney General Andrew Scott Sloan and the two Granger Roads within the state.

The case itself drew on several legal principles, including the jurisdiction of the state's highest court as well as the ability of the legislature to regulate corporations within the state according to the state constitution. In the end, the court decided in favor of the state, leaving the law in place, dealing a great blow to the railroads and handing the farmers one of their greatest victories to date in their struggle against monopolistic railroad practices. Noting the rapidly evolving atmosphere of business in the late nineteenth century, the chief justice noted, "The difficulty arises probably from applying old names to new things; applying the ancient definitions of private corporations to corporations of a character unknown when the definition arose."

Public opinion was split on the matter of the Wisconsin rail law, now being popularly referred to as the Potter Law, named for the state senator who had introduced the bill. Based on newspaper accounts from the time, it can be deduced that the argument—at least in the media—tended to fall along party lines. In an article from the *Dodgeville Chronicle* in late May, the editor made the comparison between Democratic and Republican newspapers saying, "Doesn't it sound like old times, though, to hear the Milwaukee *News* and Mineral Point *Democrat* crying out 'unconstitutional,'" and "We have yet to hear of the first Republican paper in the State of Wisconsin which either directly or indirectly opposes the enforcement of the railroad law."

Naturally, the railroads were vehemently opposed to the new law and continued their struggle against its enforcement. After numerous hearings and decisions within the Wisconsin courts, by fall the matter had been fully decided and the Potter Law was here to stay. Another letter from the CNW president to the governor, published in the *Wisconsin State Journal* in October, signaled reluctant acceptance that the fight was over and the railroads would finally comply with the law. Alex Mitchell, president of the CNW, stated, "The 'Potter Law' was without precedent in the history of any state or country, disastrous in its effects and wholly uncalled for by anything this company had done or failed to do." He also made the bold claim that "no more money can now be obtained from anyone, anywhere for the construction of railways in Wisconsin, or for the providing of equipment for existing lines, and a stoppage of many contemplated improvements has become a matter of necessity." However, Mitchell also noted that until a repeal of the law, he fully expected that he and his company would comply as law-abiding citizens.

The effort of the Grange within the enactment of the Potter Law and its subsequent legal fights cannot be understated. In a report from the *Kansas Farmer*, a Topeka paper, the Wisconsin Grange master reported on the importance of continued efforts against the railroads for the benefit of "all the industrial classes." Moreover, he noted, "Let us demand of our representatives that not only the provisions of control already secured be retained, but that such additional detailed legislation be had in this direction." He went on to call all Grange members to action in the upcoming election of 1875, urging them to elect representatives who would side with the people over business interests.

National opinion on the Potter Law was mixed, and reports began to appear that the claims being made by the railroads were potentially exaggerated. One investigation published in the *New-York Tribune* claimed that the financial losses to the CNW would be "less than one half as great as it has been asserted to be by the managers of the companies." In the same paper, a letter to the editor spoke of "the oppressed millions against the lordly, the grasping, and the swindling few." However, papers like the *Portland Daily Free Press* assailed the law and its effect on railroad expansion, claiming, "The immediate effect will be to check railroad enterprise in the West, if not all over the country, for capitalists will not place their money in the hands of those who assume to be their foes, to control."

Wisconsin's law became the flashpoint of the 1870s, heralded by the farmers as a necessary balancing of the scales and decried by the industrialists as government gone too far. The law was held up as the prime example of collective action by consumers against the emerging empires created by the railroads and their monopolistic actions. However, the greatest effect of the Granger Laws, and the Potter Law in particular, lay not in Wisconsin, Iowa, Minnesota or Illinois, but in Washington, D.C.

In January 1874, hearings were underway within the halls of the Capitol in Washington on the necessity of a commission to regulate commerce between the states, to fully exercise the so-called commerce clause in the U.S. Constitution's first article. The argument was being made that like the canal traffic, and coastal shipping before it, the national nature of the growing railroad industry meant that the only effective means to regulate these corporations was through the federal government. As reported in the *Lawrence Daily Journal*, the issue of the patchwork of state regulations was specifically listed as a concern by Senator Morton, who said, "The people of the several states acting separately would be less able to protect their rights against the power of great corporations." The western states of Wisconsin, Minnesota, Iowa and Nebraska, as well as the new Union Pacific Railroad, were specifically listed as beneficiaries of a national framework for rail legislation in the same article. This act would stall in the halls of Congress for three more years, but the seeds were planted and the state efforts to regulate railroads were standing as examples for the federal government, as well as proving their popularity among the electorate.

Meanwhile, there was a political shift happening in Wisconsin that threatened the regulatory framework that had been created by the Granger politicians of 1874. In 1875, the *State Journal* in Madison reported the final composition of the state legislature of Wisconsin. In the Senate, Republicans gained a single-seat majority, and in the Assembly, Republicans garnered a twenty-eight-seat advantage over the "Reformers," a loose coalition of Democrats, Grange members, and liberal Republicans. This move took the power to maintain the strict system of controls passed in 1874 away from Governor Taylor and the Reformers.

When the legislature began its session in 1876, among the first orders of business was the repeal of the Potter Law. As reported by the *Mineral Point Weekly Tribune*, by early February, the Vance Bill had passed the Assembly with a vote of 56–30 to repeal the Potter Law. The article cited an editorial in the *Chicago Tribune* that the law had not "enrich[ed] either the farmers or merchants…" and further that, "the law has depressed the value of produce and stopped railroad building." However, the Vance Bill left in place the railroad commission and retained the power of the rail commissioners to oversee the industry throughout the state, stopping short of a wholesale deregulation of the railroads within Wisconsin. Many of the provisions in the new act resembled those passed in other Granger states but with a step back from the draconian price controls of the Potter Law. Included were annual statistical reports, prohibitions against different rates for different shippers and forbidding consolidation of competing lines (a provision very clearly aimed at the Milwaukee Road and CNW), as well as laying out punishments for the various infractions that the railroads could incur.

The new bill, effectively a repeal of the Potter Law, was seen as a positive event, heralded by leading papers in the nation's two largest commercial cities, Chicago and New York. The *Wisconsin State Journal* characterized the new legislation as an "armistice between the two great forces of prosperity in the West." While back home in Wisconsin the mood was equally positive, the *Watertown News* noted in March 1876, "These provisions greatly ameliorate those of the 'Potter law' and some of them aim to correct the abuses common to almost all railroads, in and out of Wisconsin."

By the winter of 1876, the pendulum of railroad regulation could be said to have made its return swing toward a more moderate solution to the problems facing the farmers. The Grange was at its peak, as evidenced by the August 1876 edition of the *Western Rural*, a Chicago weekly paper aimed squarely at farmers and those living outside of the city. The paper reported on the effects of the Grange in glowing terms, going so far as to say, "A new direction has been given to public thought. Once the professional man, the bond-holder and the capitalist were the only citizens thought worthy of Government protection; now the plowholder asserts his equal right and the law-makers recognize it." The paper asserted that the Grange brought down sewing machine prices and farming implement prices, raised "the standard of political morality," created libraries and brought education to untold numbers of farmers.

However, the fight against the railroads was far from complete. In the same edition of the *Western Rural*, an article detailed the dangers of the "railroad monopoly" and the railroads' "extortions" of the farmers. The paper claimed that, had all the surplus grain from Illinois, Wisconsin and Minnesota been shipped via the rails, rather than through the Great Lakes ports, it would have cost an additional $38 million. While it is likely that these numbers are exaggerated, what can be clear is that despite laws on the books in all three of the cited states, the farmers still clearly felt, and the media was in agreement, that the railroads were antagonistic toward the grain trade. Moreover, the paper warned against the vertical monopolies being created whereby railroads controlled their own operations as well as the operations of their suppliers.

As the calendar moved from 1876 to 1877, a new storm was brewing; the railroads and the eastern capitalists were not going to sit idly by as upstart farmers and Grange members dismantled the empires they had built. If the railroads had lost control of the legislature, they would turn to another political entity, one disconnected from the whims of the public and above control by the Grange—the courts. Two court cases in Illinois—*Munn v. Illinois* and *Wabash, St. Louis & Pacific Railway v. Illinois*—would set the stage for a clash between the Granger states and the railroads they hoped to keep in check. These court cases, in which the Granger movement received its greatest challenge to date, also ushered in a new player, the federal government.

4
NATIONAL RAILROAD REFORM ARRIVES

By 1877, many of the midwestern states had adopted railroad regulations, often by this point referred to as Granger Laws. The correlation between these regulations and the popular Granger movement became associated with the railroads themselves. In 1876, the Iowa law was referred to as the "Granger Railroad Law" by the *Carthage Press*, and by the early 1900s, the collection of railroads that had taken over the majority of the trackage in the Midwest was routinely referred to as "the granger railroads" in articles by papers like the *Star Tribune* in Minneapolis. However, there were also on the horizon a set of high-profile court cases that would be associated with the movement and its targeting of railroad profiteering.

The Granger Roads were nearing their final form, the result of years of consolidation in the wake of the Civil War. As of 1875, the Chicago and North Western held over 1,900 miles of rail, more than doubling the 1865 total of 930 miles. Meanwhile, the Milwaukee Road had expanded to 1,414 miles up from 825, as reported in 1868, an increase of nearly 75 percent. Meanwhile, the more southerly Granger Roads were expanding at an equally rapid pace. The Chicago, Rock Island and Pacific had 1,003 miles of rail listed in their 1877 annual report. The Chicago, Burlington and Quincy had expanded from a mere 603 miles in 1870 to a staggering 1,343 miles by December 31, 1876.

This expansion meant that all of the Granger Roads were no longer local, intrastate railroads, but regional networks spanning multiple states.

The CNW connected parts of Nebraska, Iowa, Illinois, Wisconsin and Minnesota, while the CB&Q, mirrored by the rival Rock Island, stretched as far as Colorado by the early 1880s. By the mid-1880s, the Milwaukee Road did not yet include its famed Pacific extension but had already covered much of the upper Midwest from Chicago to the western reaches of the Dakotas. These leviathan railroads were a new monster, different from the coastal shipping companies that Congress had been regulating since the earliest days of the nineteenth century. A new corporation required new rules, but the patchwork of state regulations driven by the Grange was starting to reach the extent of its effectiveness; a national framework was needed for a national rail network. The Granger Roads were hardly alone in this rail building bonanza—according to the Census Bureau in 1925, for the decade between 1870 and 1880, the United States added 40,345 miles of rail, with growth in the "West-North-Central" region comprising the largest portion at 11,048 miles of growth.

In 1877, the Supreme Court waded into the growing tension building between the states, the ever-expanding railroads and the consumers, who were often left feeling as if they were at the mercy of railroad barons for both transportation and commerce. The court heard a trio of cases that the press dubbed the "Granger Cases." Each dealt with a slightly different aspect of the Granger Laws across the upper Midwest. The Illinois case, *Munn v. Illinois*, dealt with whether or not private companies were able to be regulated as public goods. The Wisconsin case, according to the *West-Jersey Pioneer*, centered on whether the state's price setting interfered with Congress's right to regulate interstate commerce, and the Iowa case centered on creating stratified classes of rail cargo. In each case, the Supreme Court held in favor of the Granger laws, boosting the rights of the state to control the growing corporations within their territories.

Supreme Court Chief Justice Waite, 1873. *Library of Congress.*

At hand in *Munn v. Illinois* was a case that stemmed from the 1871 Illinois railroad regulations, through which the proprietors of the Munn and Scott grain elevator were charged with rate violations. The company appealed the conviction to the U.S. Supreme Court after losing in the state supreme court. According to the opinion of the court, Munn and Scott had three constitutional objects: (1) that the law violated the Constitution's provision that interstate commerce was a power of the U.S. Congress and not Illinois, (2) that this law violated the prohibition against regulatory preference of one port over another and (3) that it violated their Fourteenth Amendment due process rights by depriving them of life, liberty or property without due process.

In the end, the Supreme Court found in favor of the state. Chief Justice Waite addressed the issue of the Fourteenth Amendment, saying that price regulations are not a form of deprivation, and then addressed the very heart of the issue, whether or not a private business is private property when it operates in a public interest. To this question, Chief Justice Waite answered:

> *When, therefore, one devotes his property to a use in which the public has an interest, he, in effect, grants to the public an interest in that use, and must submit to be controlled by the public for the common good.*

This momentous decision was a watershed moment in the regulation of industry and was a victory for the Granger ideals of regulation of business for the public good.

The next case to reach the court was Chicago, Burlington and Quincy's lawsuit against Iowa on behalf of the absorbed Burlington and Missouri Railroad. The question regarded Iowa's classification of railroads and whether or not this classification was a violation of the railroad's rights to not have laws that favored one individual (or in this case, corporation, over another). Justice Waite noted:

> *It is very clear that a uniform rate of charges for all railroad companies in the state might operate unjustly upon some. It was proper therefore to provide in some way for an adaptation of the rates to the circumstances of the different roads, and the general assembly, in the exercise of its legislative discretion, has been fit to do this by a system of classification.*

The Iowa case thus decided, with the CB&Q losing their fight with the state, it was left to the CNW and their fight against the State of

Wisconsin. This case, called *Peik v. Chicago and North Western Railway Company*, rather than alleging that the law was unconstitutional, alleged that the railroads held the right to collect more than the maximum rates, when it was reasonable. The reason for this otherwise strange claim was that the charter for the CNW gave the railroad the right to "demand and receive such sum or sums of money for the transportation of persons or property…as it shall deem reasonable." However, the court ruled that the nature of the charter was amendable by future legislation per the Wisconsin constitution. A second argument in the Wisconsin case alleged that the railroad was immune from regulations by Wisconsin since only Congress had the ability to regulate interstate commerce. Justice Waite, in clear terms, foreshadowed events to come, saying, "Until Congress acts in reference to the relations of this company to interstate commerce, it is certainly within the power of Wisconsin to regulate its fares, &c., so far as they are of domestic concern."

Media responded to the cases with praise—an August 1877 article in the *Lawrence Standard* stated of the decision, "The bearing upon our local cause here seems to us to be direct, and to clearly affirm the power of the State to fix maximum rates…the Legislature owes it to the people to apply at the earliest possible moment." The aforementioned article about the Granger cases in the *West-Jersey Pioneer* was equally effusive, declaring the decisions' "importance can hardly be underestimated." Likewise, the *Morning Times* of

Railroad map of the United States, 1877. *David Rumsey Map Archive.*

Oakland remarked about the excitement surrounding these cases, saying, "The great agricultural States were in a condition bordering on rebellion, so fierce was the excitement….We believe justice will be done to people and corporations, too."

Thus, entering the 1880s, the states' right to regulate the fares of railroads through their constitutional police powers was safe, and thanks in large part to the efforts of the Grange, people were for the time being free from oppressive railroad fares. However, one aspect of the railroads' operations became clear in the process of litigating these cases: the character of much of their business was now in the interest of the federal government rather than only within each of the states. Yet the federal government was still some distance away from enacting any legislation, still embroiled in the tumultuous Reconstruction era following the Civil War.

Appropriately, the next major movement in the push for federal railroad regulation came from another Granger state, Illinois. At the heart of the 1886 legal case that ensued were two shipments of grain from two different cities in Illinois to New York. The Wabash, St. Louis and Pacific railway charged two customers, one from Gilman and another from Peoria, different rates, which the statutes of Illinois forbade. This time, the court, in a shocking about-face within the span of less than a decade, reversed course from the 1877 Granger cases and declared that, since railroads were doing business across state lines, they could no longer discriminate in their rates, so long as those rates included interstate carriage. The stage was set: the Interstate Commerce bill that had been introduced years prior suddenly came back to the forefront.

In December 1886, within only two months of the decision on Wabash, the Interstate Commerce Act reached floor debates in the U.S. Senate. It should come as no surprise that a senator from the midwestern Granger state of Iowa made its most impassioned plea. As reported in the *Inter Ocean* newspaper of Chicago, Senator James F. Wilson of Iowa pleaded with his fellow senators, saying, "For ten years and more we have debated, now let us act." Wilson further illustrated the point by showing that it was more profitable for farmers to ship grain from western Iowa to Chicago rather than to eastern Iowa during a crop shortage in the state.

According to the Bureau of Economic Research, the debate on the bill continued into the middle of January as the Senate debated, amended and reamended the version of the bill that had passed the House of Representatives back in July. The revised version of the bill passed in the Senate with an overwhelming majority; the final roll call in the upper chamber was 43 in favor and 15 opposed. The bill now faced another vote in the House before being sent to President Grover Cleveland. The House took little time to consider the new bill, and only a week after the Senate passage, the House voted 219 to 41 to pass United States Chapter 104 An Act to Regulate Commerce, ending the debate and signaling a huge win for the Grangers and farmers across the nation.

The act mimicked many of the laws passed in the Granger states. Again, rates were limited to those that were "reasonable and just," as well as outlawing "undue or unreasonable preference or advantage to any person, company, firm, corporation or locality, or any other particular description of traffic." The act provided for significant penalties for the breach of the act—up to a maximum $5,000 fine for each infraction. In another facsimile of the Granger-sponsored laws, in order to provide for enforcement, the act set up the Interstate Commerce Commission to check for violations and to monitor the enforcement of the new act.

This commission grew to become one of the most powerful forces acting on the railroads and highways of the nation, thanks in large part to the example laid down by the Granger legislation in the Midwest. The Interstate Commerce Commission, or ICC, was composed of five members who served rotating six-year terms so that in any given year only one of the five was a potentially new member. These commissioners were appointed by the president and confirmed by the Senate. The ICC had the power to issue subpoenas and require annual reports, as well as investigate the operations of any railroad that fell within its jurisdiction—that is, any railroad that operated business across state lines. The commission was also required to compile an annual report of its own, to be forwarded on to Congress.

However, outside of the Granger states, the mood regarding national legislation to control commerce was not as widely praised. In the *San Francisco Examiner*, the mood was gloomy regarding the implementation of the bill, reading, "Our Merchants Dreading the Inter-State Commerce Law," and "The interstate commerce railroad law, which goes into effect two weeks hence, is regarded with considerable anxiety by the merchants of San Francisco." Likewise, the *Perry County Monitor and Sun* reported in late April 1887, "The Inter-State Commerce Commission is constantly deluged with letters from representatives of various interests throughout the country complaining of hardships inflicted by the enforcement of the act." It would seem then, that beyond the home territory of the Grangers, the support for railroad regulation may have been lacking.

Of particular concern in the South was the fourth section of the law, which forbade charging less for long-haul trips than short-haul trips, provided they were along the same line; in other words, railroads needed to charge a flat rate per mile no matter how far the freight traveled. This particular facet of the law was crucial to the farmers in the Midwest, as this was seen as one of the primary ways that the railroads abused farmers who primarily were engaged in short-haul local freight. The *Topeka Daily Capital* reported that within the first days of April, delegations from southern states were already in Washington petitioning the newly established commission for a temporary suspension of section 4 of the Interstate Commerce Act, reporting that they were out of necessity raising their long-distance rates to be equal to their short-distance rates so as not to lose money over the shorter, and more costly, routes. This reality had not escaped those in the Midwest either, with the *Jasper Weekly Courier* reporting, "Revised freight tariffs are going to work ruin to the Southern shippers." In the end, the contentious section 4 was left alone by the ICC, as reported in the *Blue Mound Sun*: "Railroad companies must judge for themselves as to whether they are entitled to discriminate under presumed conditions, when aggrieved parties can seek redress from the Commission."

Nevertheless, the Commission charged on in its work. In July, the *Bloomfield Vindicator* reported that a "bureau of statistics" had been created by the commission to track the statistics of the hundreds of corporations it was charged with monitoring. Around the same time, it was reported in the *Wilson County Citizen* that the ICC held that "commercial passengers" could not be given special preference through rail passes that offered a lower rate per mile than standard passenger tickets. Yet even while the ICC was finding its legs, there were other pieces of legislation in the works that threatened to further restrain the powers of the ever-growing railroad corporations.

Only three years after the passage of the Interstate Commerce Act, Congress passed a new law aimed not at regulation of prices or fares but at the issue of monopoly itself. In 1890, the Sherman Antitrust Act came into force, aimed at dissolving the powerful and dangerous monopolies instead of simply curbing their effects. This act was passed with awe-inspiring bipartisan support, with only a single dissenting vote between both houses. Now the federal government was equipped with the weapon it needed to not only limit the likes of Rockefeller, Carnegie and Vanderbilt but also completely dismantle the empires they had worked so hard to build.

Public reaction was more mixed when it came to the antitrust act. The *Champaign Daily Gazette*, a paper firmly in Granger territory, characterized

Supplement to No. 418.
NAVY.
WAR.
IT IS THE DUTY OF THO
TO CLOSELY LIMIT PUB
OF THE GOVERNME
J. Keppler.
W. C. Whitney, Secretary of the Navy.
Daniel Manning, Secretary of the Treasury.
A. H. Garland, Attorney-General.
T. F. Bayard, Secretary of State.
PRESIDENT CLEVEL

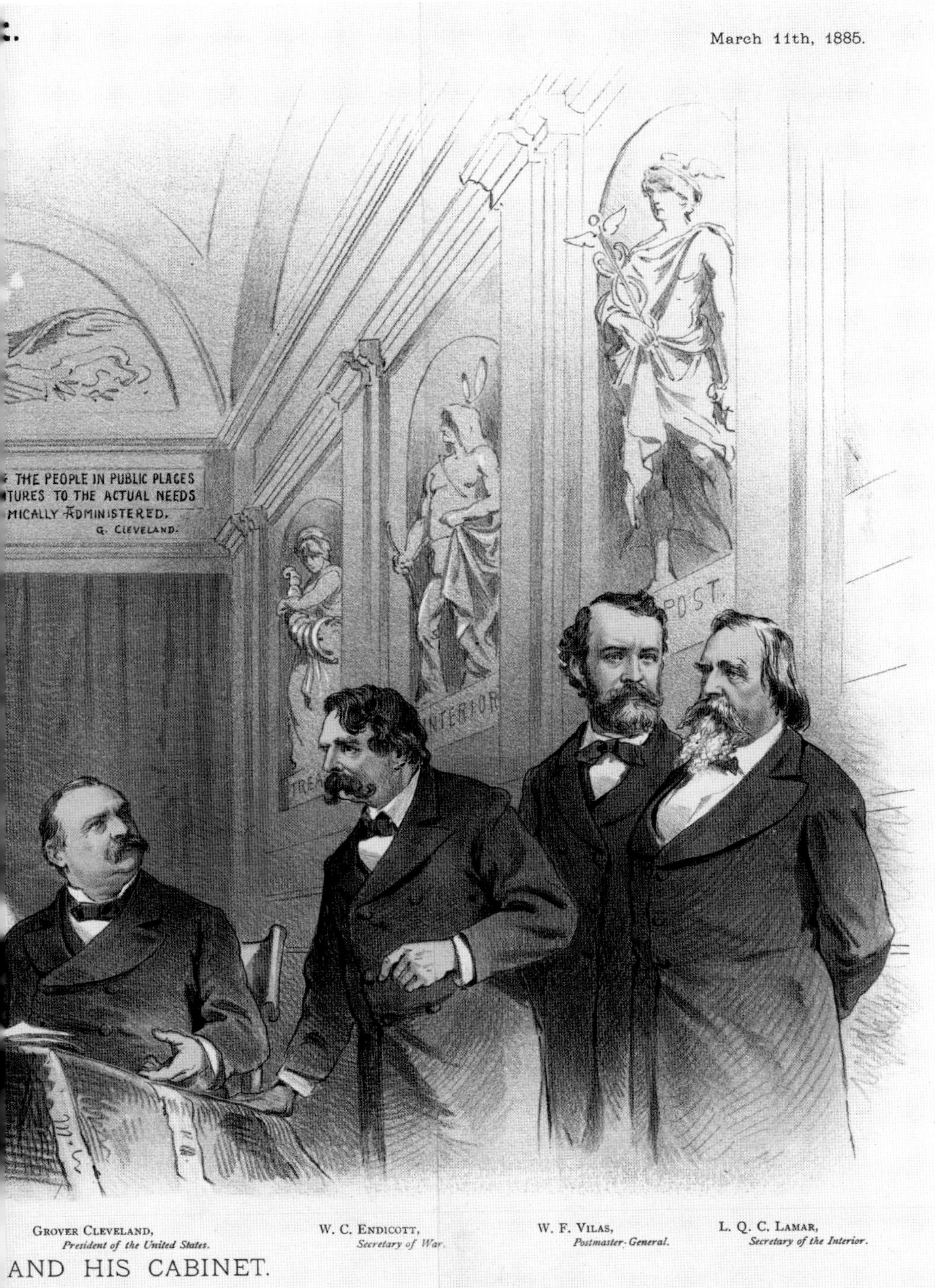

U.S. President Grover Cleveland and his cabinet. *Library of Congress.*

Political cartoon with Uncle Sam standing in as the Interstate Commerce Commission. *Library of Congress.*

Political cartoon titled "The Modern Colossus of Rail," in reference to William Henry Vanderbilt. *Library of Congress.*

the act as "somewhat drastic" and did mention that "Business Men Will Be Happy." The Sherman Antitrust Act followed a similar path as the Interstate Commerce Act, from state experimentation to national legislation. According to research from Wayne Collins in the *Fordham Law Review*, there were thirteen states—including Iowa, North and South Dakota, Nebraska, Kansas, Missouri, and Michigan—that had passed intrastate antitrust laws by 1890, further demonstrating the fertile ground that existed in the Midwest states for business regulation.

The landmark law outlawed any "contract, combination in the form of trust or otherwise, or conspiracy, in restraint of trade or commerce," as well as giving the right to those who felt they were affected by a trust to sue and receive "threefold" the amount of money they felt they lost to the trust or monopoly. The punishment for those found guilty of breach of the law was severe as well, set at $5,000 and/or a year in prison. The law was clear: the federal government was not going to stand for any sort of business that attempted to limit competition. The Sherman Act's close succession to the Interstate Commerce Act can lead one to believe that the federal government was taking a strong stand in support of the consumer over the businessman, signaling a departure from the laissez-faire economics of the first century of U.S. history. However, the great equalizing force of the Supreme Court in U.S. politics stepped in within a few short years and returned the status quo.

In 1895, the Supreme Court heard arguments in the case of *United States v. E.C. Knight*. This was the first major legal challenge to the Sherman Antitrust law. In the case, the American Sugar Refining Company of New Jersey was accused of creating a trust to control the trade in refined sugar within the United States, in violation of the Sherman Antitrust law. In the court's opinion, it was admitted that the American Sugar Refining Company controlled all but five sugar refineries in the United States; however, in the majority opinion given by Chief Justice Fuller, the court decided, "There was nothing in the proofs to indicate any intention to put a restraint upon trade or commerce, and the fact, as we have seen, that trade or commerce might be indirectly affected was not enough to entitle complainants to a decree." In essence, the court decided that although the sugar trade was most definitely controlled nearly entirely by the American Sugar Refining Company, they didn't attempt to restrain trade or unduly change the market through their power, and therefore their monopoly was still legal.

The judicial rollback was not limited to the Sherman Act; in cases reaching nearly into the twentieth century, the court slowly eroded the capability of the Interstate Commerce Act to do the work it had been created for. However, by the 1890s, Congress had been working to further enhance the abilities of the ICC, adding railroad safety to the list of its responsibilities in 1893 with the passage of the Railroad Safety on March 2. This act mandated safety features in trains such as automatic train brakes (those not requiring manual application by a brakeman), grab handles on each car and a standard drawbar for all cars across the nation. Perhaps most important, however, was the use of the ICC to handle any violations of the law and to set the standards as suggested by the American Railway Association. Yet in two cases in the 1890s, the court dismantled two of the most important powers of the ICC.

The first crack in the façade of the act formed in 1897 in the case *of ICC v. Cincinnati, N.O. & Texas Pacific Railway Company*. The question at hand in this case was whether Congress had granted the ICC the power to fix rates or simply enforce penalties when rates were deemed unreasonable. The argument largely boiled down to the legislative language and whether or not the law was written such that the ICC could "fix rates," whereas other states' railroad regulations did indeed include that language. As a result, the court struck down the ICC's ability to set rates for future use and its ability to seek court injunctions to force the hand of a railroad to set a particular rate.

The next case also arose in 1897, between the ICC and the Alabama Midland Railway. This time, the case involved the ever-controversial section 4 prohibition against rate discrimination between short and long-haul routes. The Supreme Court held that the courts are able to further weigh evidence as to the factual context of the breach of the law and to thus overrule the ICC when it comes to matters arising from a suit brought against a road. Further, the court alleged that in this case, there was sufficient evidence to overrule the finding of the ICC and render the case moot. It should be mentioned that Justice Harlan offered a scathing dissent, wherein he accused the court of rendering "the Commission a useless body." Thus, the ICC, now stripped of its ability to enforce two of its most basic charges, but now the overseer of railroad safety, entered the twentieth century—a century with the railroads growing ever larger and more powerful but with a government largely unable to check their progress.

While the nation, split along primarily regional lines, continued to argue over how the federal government would or could regulate business, the Granger Roads continued to grow. While the railroads of the Midwest were involved, sometimes critically in lobbying against legislation and the legal cases that defined the late nineteenth century, this didn't seem to slow them down.

Supreme Court Chief Justice John Marshall Harlan. *Library of Congress.*

In the last years of the nineteenth century, the Granger Roads were at their most powerful point to date. The Milwaukee Road reported a net earnings of $14.5 million in their 1899 annual report. This was in stark contrast to their 1877 earnings, which barely surpassed $3 million. There is likewise a similar gulf between the track mileage in 1877 and 1899 for the Milwaukee Road. In 1877, the company, along with its subsidiaries, claimed 1,400 of track across the four states of Wisconsin, Minnesota, Illinois and Iowa, whereas in 1899, the company controlled 8,006 miles of track, more than quadrupling their trackage in the time between the *Munn* decision and the neutering of the ICC. The Milwaukee Road was busy snapping up the competition as well. In 1890, the purchase of the Milwaukee and Northern Railroad was announced in the *Weekly Wisconsin*; with the addition of this line, the Milwaukee Road added connections up the western coast of Wisconsin and into the Upper Peninsula of Michigan.

Likewise, the CB&Q saw tremendous growth. In 1877, the road stated in their annual report a net earnings of $5.18 million and a total trackage of only 1,343 miles. This put it in proximity to the Milwaukee Road in terms of earnings and mileage as of 1877. In 1901, as reported in the 1902 annual report, the net income for the road was $15.9 million, and the total track miles that the CB&Q controlled was 7,736 miles. Both of these, when accounting for the extra two years of growth, also show that the CB&Q was pacing the same rapid growth as the Milwaukee Road in this time. While the Milwaukee Road was busy expanding and buying other railroads, the CB&Q was attempting a merger on a more co-equal basis. The first major acquisition was the Burlington and Missouri Railroad in 1884, as it was included in the 1884 annual report. Following this, however, the railroad looked not toward smaller or inferior roads to absorb but to a partner to merge with. The Great Northern and Union Pacific Railroads were both considered, but in 1901, it was reported in the *Missoulian* newspaper that

James Hill, owner of the Great Northern, would be purchasing a stake in the CB&Q road and running it alongside his already established network.

The Rock Island, ever the mirror of the CB&Q, was growing apace during the same period. In 1877, the Rock Island generated $3.38 million in net earnings from 1,003 miles of railroad. However, as it was to its fellow Granger Roads, the period of national regulation was kind to the Rock Island. By 1900, the Rock Island was earning $7.68 million from its expanded network of 2,955 miles. While the gains made by the Rock Island were not as dramatic as the CB&Q or Milwaukee Road, the railroad still doubled its net income and nearly tripled its available track within less than a quarter decade. It should be noted the Rock Island did not have the same level of major mergers and acquisitions as the other Granger Roads in the 1880s or 1890s; it simply grew through construction and sound management practices.

The Chicago and North Western was equally as prosperous in the late nineteenth century. As of 1899, the road claimed in its annual report an average of 5,076 miles operated and a net income of over $13 million before costs incurred from dividends and interest. This stands in contrast to the 1,499 miles and $4.7 million reported in 1875, putting it firmly in the same league as the Milwaukee Road and CB&Q and outpacing the Rock Island. The CNW could not point to its own organic expansion as the source of the massive growth it achieved by 1899. The CNW, in keeping with its history to this point, absorbed multiple railroads in the late nineteenth century. In June 1880, the *Racine Journal* reported the CNW was managing the Sioux City and Pacific Railroad; in September 1884, the Freemont, Elkhorn and Missouri Valley was taken over, later to be absorbed completely; and the Milwaukee and Lake Shore line was fully absorbed in 1893.

It is safe to say then that despite numerous legal challenges and hostile attitudes from the farmers they served, the Granger Roads were not only surviving the tumultuous first attempts at national regulation but also thriving more than they had in the years before regulation.

The pace at which the Granger Roads were merging with other roads, whether through mutual choice or through a hostile takeover, certainly would have drawn the ire of the federal government had the courts not dismantled the very instruments that the legislative branch had created to prevent such combinations. The governments of the various Granger states had once been the ultimate protectors of the farmers, but in the new era of national legislation, they had to stand by and watch their legacy be dismantled, able only to legislate those railroads that were entirely within their borders.

The Granger Roads had grown beyond the control of the states and were operating under a court system unwilling to rein them in. Despite the best efforts of the Grangers, with so much promise in the 1870s, it seemed as if the railroads had come out of the first major period of railroad legislation none the worse.

The situation was no different throughout the rest of the nation. With the nation deep in the Gilded Age, opulent wealth and robber barons were the norm, and government intervention was the exception. According to the Census Bureau's report *Historical Statistics of the United States 1789–1945*, transportation in 1869 brought in payments of $718 million, whereas the valuation in 1900 was $1.6 billion. Similar trends were reported for manufacturing, which rose from $1 billion to $2.9 billion over the same period, and mining and quarrying, which saw a more than fourfold increase from $102 million to $453 million. Business was booming, and it appeared to most as if there was no reason to change the status quo. Many around the nation were excited to put the hard times of the Panic of 1873 behind them. An article in the *Salt Lake Herald* spoke of "a revival of business prosperity" and "a unanimous change for the better." It seemed as if the nation had righted itself. With the tough years of Reconstruction and the economic uncertainty that followed the Civil War over, Americans could look toward the dawn of a new century with optimism.

Yet there was also a new period of legislative fervor dawning. On the horizon, new elements of society were clamoring for change. A new generation of journalists was beginning to comment on the seedy underbelly of society. Names like Ida Tarbell would step into the limelight, shining a painful beam on the economic evil of monopolies. Upton Sinclair wrote his famous exposé of the food industry, especially the abuses of the meat industry with its epicenter in the railroad city of Chicago. Perhaps most importantly for the story of the Granger Roads, this new wave of optimism for societal change found a cheerleader from the Midwest, a governor from Wisconsin who would soon become the poster child for the Progressive Era, Robert La Follette.

The Progressive Era saw a revival of the ideals that Congress had espoused when they created the ICC and the Sherman Antitrust Act, but perhaps most importantly, this time the progressives had learned from their mistakes and worked to ensure that the new systems they put in place to regulate society's evils would not be dismantled from the bench.

5

THE PROGRESSIVE ERA AND ADVENT OF THE AUTOMOBILE

As the nineteenth century turned to the twentieth, an era of technological and social innovation was dawning. In a few short decades, the railroads would go from having a stranglehold on motorized transportation to being just one of multiple forms of transportation that would dilute the pool of available freight, mail and passengers to be carried. Similarly, the economic ideals of the late Reconstruction period emerged again as a new wave of support for government-driven solutions to social ills became the rage within the United States. No longer was the public content to allow the businessmen of America to control the machinations in Washington, D.C. In only two decades, the world that the Granger railroads had been so prosperous in ground to a halt, and despite appearing at their greatest, it was the beginning of the end for the four great roads of the Midwest, a process they had unknowingly kicked off in the 1870s.

The first tremor to shake the foundations of the railroad's dominance was the foundation of the gas-powered automobile industry within the United States. While Daimler had created the first gasoline internal combustion vehicle in Germany in the 1880s, it was not until 1896 that a company was able to successfully design, build and sell a gas-powered vehicle in the United States. Perhaps fittingly, the Duryea Motor Wagon Company built its vehicles in Peoria, Illinois, right in the heart of Granger territory. Duryea Motor Wagons won acclaim by competing in various competitions, including one in Chicago in 1895, according to the *Hawaiian Gazette*, in which the Duryea design won a race covering fifty-four miles in eight hours. By 1897, the Duryea Motor Wagon company was selling its designs for $1,500, as advertised in the *Berkshire Eagle*, which described one vehicle as "the toppiest thing that the swells can be seen in." In 1905, two teams of men set out in Oldsmobile Runabouts to test the viability of driving from New York to Portland Oregon, a trip previously only possible by rail. It took the winning vehicle forty-four days, but in doing so, the trip proved to the American public that cars were more than a fad.

As personal vehicles became more popular and their commercial viability was proven, more companies were founded, and by 1913, there was one registered automobile to every seventy-seven Americans. Brands like Ford, Chevrolet, Duesenberg, Olds and Buick became household names, and Detroit became the center of a blossoming motor vehicle industry. One issue that held back the automotive industry, however, was the poor state of roads within the United States. The first published highway map of Wisconsin, for instance, was produced in 1916 and noted "secondary lines of travel of doubtful passability in certain seasons." On a federal level, the Office of Road Inquiry did not become the Bureau of Public Roads until 1921, showing that the state of road travel in the United States was far behind that of rail travel but was quickly catching up in the early twentieth century. While the automobile offered individuals freedom of movement the railroads, tied

A "horseless carriage" similar to the Duryea Motor Wagon. *Library of Congress.*

to their set routes, couldn't match, another new invention was coming that would rival the railroads' ability to move parcels and mail at speed across the great expanses of the growing nation.

In 1903, on the dunes of Kitty Hawk, North Carolina, two brothers achieved the first powered flight of a heavier-than-air vehicle. Powered by a small gasoline engine pushing a propeller and covered in canvas, the Wright Flyer, as it was known, would not have seemed a threat to the great steel behemoths of the railroad. The Wright brothers' first flight was only 120 feet, and the longest of that first day lasted barely longer than 800 feet, less than a mile in total for an aircraft that could hold only one man aloft. However, much like the fledgling automobile industry, the new aircraft grew by leaps and bounds, helped significantly by the innovation of the Great War air forces. Within only fifteen years of the invention of the airplane, the first U.S. Air-Mail contracts were being awarded for flights between Washington, D.C., and New York City. These mail contracts foreshadowed future competition between air and rail for connecting the two coasts of the nation.

In 1900, the United States was still sparsely populated, and while the great cities of the East still held sway, the population had begun to shift farther west and into the cities. There were, as of 1900, forty-five states, with Arizona, New Mexico and Oklahoma yet to attain statehood in the continental United States. The nation was still heavily reliant on rail transportation to facilitate the movement of people and material, especially between the developing West Coast cities and the more settled areas in the Midwest and East. The relative inefficiency of early road vehicles was compounded by the lack of any sort of wide-scale gasoline vehicle infrastructure, and airplanes were simply too light and too dangerous in the early days of aviation to be any real threat to the railroads for anything other than express mail services.

As a result, the railroads continued their expansion and consolidation. In the last twenty years of the nineteenth century, aided by relaxed regulations, the railroads experienced a building boom that had not been seen since their inception. Railroad construction data from the Bureau of Economic Research shows that the previous peak had been reached in 1872, the year before the Panic of 1873, when 7,439 miles of track were laid nationwide. That record was surpassed in 1881 with over 9,000 miles laid, and then the railroads pushed their building spree even further in 1887 with a staggering 13,810 miles of rail laid in a single year. Period rail network maps show a dizzying array of interconnected and often competing rail lines from the

Granger states eastward, while the western networks were primarily laid north to south with a handful of transcontinental routes connecting the two halves of the nation.

However, as the railroads were beginning to reach their greatest power, both in terms of mileage and economic impact, the attitude in Washington was changing. The 1900s were a time of massive change in the United States; record immigration was changing the population balance within the country. Whereas previous waves of immigrants had, as in the settling of the Granger states, pushed westward into the frontier, the new waves were settling largely within cities. The 1900 U.S. Census showed thirty-eight cities that had more than 100,000 inhabitants, up from twenty-eight in 1890. The nation was also beginning to find its footing internationally. Having defeated Spain in the Spanish-American War in 1898, the nation now had its first overseas territory in the Philippines as well as a protectorate in Cuba. These new markets were now open to American goods, and it was the rails that moved these goods from the interior to the coasts for shipment abroad.

Yet as was often the case in the United States in this period, the prosperity was only surface-deep, and much like the Panic of 1873, which drove the first rise of the Granger movement, another panic, this time in 1893, saw the return of the ideals that had been abandoned in the late 1870s and

Orville and Wilbur Wright's "Wright Flyer" at Kitty Hawk. *Library of Congress.*

Mechanics of the U.S. Air Service, 1918. *Library of Congress.*

1880s. Once again, farmers saw a depression that caused their crop prices to plummet. The resultant depression brought farmers and their livelihood to the fore again. As in the late 1860s and 1870s, overproduction was to blame, and despite efforts to encourage government interventions, none came, and the farmers were left to organize themselves again.

This time, the farmers turned not to the Grange but to the formation of their own political party, designed to take their issues and interests to every level of government. In 1892, a convention was held in Omaha, Nebraska, and the new Populist Party issued its platform, a manifesto of their beliefs and the solutions for what ailed the farmer and the laborer alike. The so-called Omaha Platform listed among the chief complaints the poor monetary policies of the United States, which limited currency and kept interest rates high, as the nation was still using gold to back each dollar. While monetary policy and the immense debate that raged around it at the end of the nineteenth century is beyond the scope of this book, it is important to note that in the Midwest the debate over silver coinage was meant to facilitate easy access to new currency for struggling farmers.

The Populist movement, the spiritual successor to the Grangers, was certainly extreme in its demands but understood that the government up through 1892 was unable or unwilling to achieve the ends they desired, stating:

> *We believe that the power of government—in other words, of the people—should be expanded (as in the case of the postal service) as rapidly and as far as the good sense of an intelligent people and the teaching of experience shall justify, to the end that oppression, injustice, and poverty shall eventually cease in the land.*

Beyond expanding the scope and power of government, the Populist movement was clear: there was one industry in particular it desired the government to rein in—the railroads. The third declaration of the platform stated, "We believe that the time has come when the railroad corporations will either own the people or the people must own the railroads; and, should the government enter upon the work of owning and managing all railroads, we should favor an amendment to the constitution by which all people engaged in the government service shall be placed under a civil-service regulation of the most rigid character, so as to prevent the increase of the power of the national administration by the use of such additional government employees."

The Populist Party raced to prominence in 1892, running numerous local and state candidates and even a third-party candidate for president. However, despite strong showings as a third party in 1892 and a shared second place in 1896, courtesy of both the Democratic Party and People's Party nominating the same candidate, the Populists could not overcome the Republican strongholds in the Northeast and Midwest. However, it was the movement among the middle and lower classes of society that would translate itself into more concrete action in the following decade.

In the presidential election of 1900, William McKinley won a second term as president over perennial challenger and occasional Populist William Jennings Bryan. Yet it was not the policies of either McKinley or Bryan that would shape the decade to come but those of New York governor and vice-presidential candidate Theodore Roosevelt. While President McKinley was speaking at the Pan-American Exposition in Buffalo, New York, an anarchist named Leon Czolgosz approached McKinley during a meet-and-greet and shot him twice in the abdomen. Despite appearing to recover, within eight days, the president had died, the second president to die at the hands of an assassin within only fifty years. What Czolgosz couldn't have known was the chain of events he set off by moving Theodore "Teddy" Roosevelt from the office of vice president to the leader of the nation.

President Roosevelt has long been considered one of the great figures of the Progressive Era, and he wasted little time in establishing himself as a man who would bring vitality back to the withering regulatory acts of the 1870s and 1880s. As had been the case for many of the major events regarding railroad regulation, a Granger Road was right in the thick of the fight. In March 1902, a suit was brought against the Northern Security Company under the provisions of the Sherman Antitrust Act. The Northern Securities Company had been created by E.H. Harriman and J.P. Morgan in order to combine the stock of the Great Northern Railroad, previously mentioned for its combination with the CB&Q Railroad and the Northern Pacific Railroad, as a new company that could hold the majority of the stock of both companies, thereby essentially consolidating the two railroads under one holding company but leaving both otherwise independent of each other. As these railroads were both roughly parallel to each other, it became clear that this combination would remove competition, akin to what the Sherman antitrust bill had hoped to prevent.

According to an article in the *Eagle River Review* in March 1902, the suit claimed it was "a policy which would promote the interests, not of one system at the expense of the other, but of both at the expense of the public." Furthermore, the article quoted the suit as saying, "If the government fails to prevent the carrying out of this combination or conspiracy…indeed the entire railway systems of the nation may be absorbed, merged, and consolidated, thus placing the public at the absolute mercy of the holding corporation." Shortly after that the company sued, and once again the Supreme Court was called on to be the arbiter in the struggle between the great railroad interests, this time again in the Midwest, and a federal government being driven to rein them in.

It took another two years, but in a landmark reversal of fortune for the railroad interests, the Supreme Court found in favor of the U.S. government in a 5–4 decision. Justice Harlan stated in his opinion:

> *The Circuit Court was undoubtedly right when it said—all the Judges of that court concurring—that the combination referred to led inevitably to the following results: first, it placed the control of the two roads in the hands of a single person, to-wit, the Securities Company, by virtue of its ownership*

> *of a large majority of the stock of both companies; second, it destroyed every motive for competition between two roads engaged in interstate traffic, which were natural competitors for business, by pooling the earnings of the two roads for the common benefit of the stockholders of both companies.*

The decision in the Northern Securities case was a massive win for the Progressive movement, the natural outgrowth of the Populist movement of the 1890s. Public reaction was immediate and overwhelmingly positive. The *Chippewa Herald Telegram* reported, "Messages of congratulation from all parts of the country are being delivered to President Roosevelt by telegraph, by mail, and in person on the Supreme Court decision in the Northern Securities Case." Even traditionally commerce-friendly states like California commended the act, with the *San Francisco Examiner* reporting, "No valid objection can be made to the decree below in form or in substance."

Even by 1904, it was clear that a new day was dawning and that the president was not going to go easy on the trusts. In 1904, Attorney General Philander Knox was offered a position as a U.S. senator. An article was published in the *Dispatch*, a Moline, Illinois paper, about what that would mean for the nation, as Knox had been leading the legal crusade against the trusts on behalf of the president. Knox was quoted as saying, "President Roosevelt's anti-trust policies are his own, and my leaving his cabinet can have no conceivable effect on them." Later in the article, the view that many in the Midwest held was revealed when the

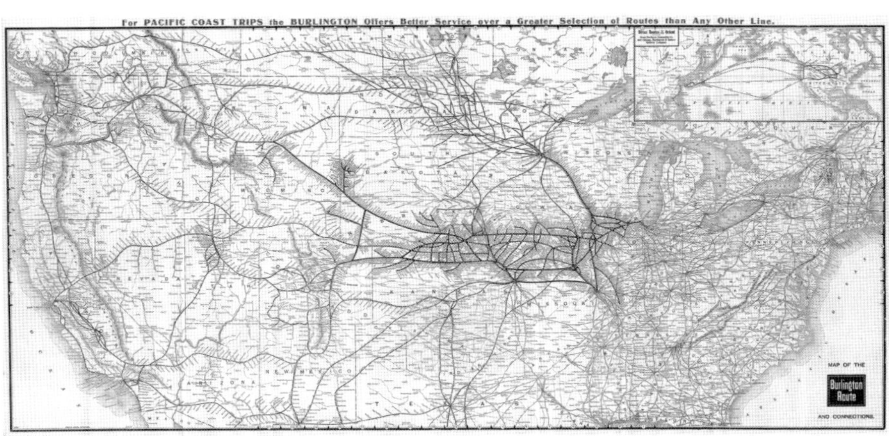

Chicago, Burlington, and Quincy network map, 1907. *David Rumsey Map Archive.*

interviewer asked Knox if it was because of his fight against the trusts that the moneyed interests had him transferred to the Senate, where he would be less able to harm them. Knox responded with incredulity, saying, "I resent the imputation that I am a man who can be cajoled into abandoning a line of action for which I have been pursuing." The message being sent was clear: the president was a man of the people, and the federal government, now with the full backing of the court, was turning a new page and business would be subservient to Congress and not the other way around.

Roosevelt and the Populists in Congress weren't done yet, however, and after reinvigorating the Sherman Antitrust Act, they turned their attention to another key instrument against the industry that the Granger railroads and the Supreme Court had neutered, the Interstate Commerce Commission. Introduced in early 1906, the Hepburn Act hoped to address the major pitfall the court had seized on in removing the ICC's ability to set maximum rates by adding language that would allow the ICC to do just that. Roosevelt was a strong proponent of the bill, which, after some debate, cleared the house in its original form. However, on reaching the U.S. Senate, the bill began to stall. Debate raged, even among the Progressives, with one article in *Capper's Weekly*, a Topeka paper, recounting a particularly vociferous disagreement between Senator Robert La Follette of Wisconsin and Senator Chester Long of Kansas in which Senator Long called La Follette a "political faker" as well as charging him with being out of line with Roosevelt's progressive ideas on the bill.

Naturally, the Hepburn Act came from the Granger states, this time introduced by Iowa Representative William P. Hepburn. Hepburn said of his namesake act, "[This legislation] will aid toward minifying a number of wrongs; it will give greater contentment to all the people in the belief that they are not being made the puppet and the football of [railroad] carriers." The act was, in reality, an expansion of an earlier attempt at reinvigorating the ICC called the Elkins Act, which forbade the practice of rate rebates, essentially allowing large shippers to have lower rates than small shippers. This process was one that many of the Granger laws, and the original Interstate Commerce Act, had hoped to address directly. The debate over the bill was fierce and long-lasting, with the Speaker of the House reportedly telling a conference committee in late June 1906 to "stay in session until its work is completed," according to reports in the *Daily Nonpareil*. In the end, at nearly midnight on June 29, the Senate relented and passed the act, with the president signing it shortly thereafter.

Public opinion of the passage was generally positive, despite it being somewhat overshadowed by concurrent discussions of the Pure Food and Drug Act, one of the crowning achievements of the Progressive Era. In the *Washington Times*, on July 1, the act was called "the great and distinguishing achievement of the session," while the *Brooklyn Daily Eagle* said of the bill, "Foremost in importance among the legislation enacted by the Fifty-ninth Congress is the so-called Hepburn Bill…not only for the evils it seeks to correct, but also because it proved to be the entering wedge for subsequent corrective legislation." Even western states, traditionally in favor of less regulation over the railroads, which were their connection to the markets east, seemed to be in favor, with the *Ranch*, a Seattle, Washington paper, noting, "Somebody must have the power to break such a combination. The rate bill will do that and such an action will be right." Yet the entire nation, even within the Midwest, should not be characterized as entirely in favor. The *Southwestern Grain and Flour Journal*, for instance, said of the bill, "The rate bill as finally passed both houses of congress will serve and an instrument to fool the people good and hard for a few years to come." However, it should be noted that much of the opposition in the aforementioned article was due to a belief that the bill was approved by the corporations and that many of the provisions in the law could and likely would be challenged in court and the railroads would continue to do their business as they had unhindered at the cost of the people.

The ICC was renewed and growing in power, but Congress was not yet done repairing and reinforcing the commission, even without the guiding force of Teddy Roosevelt as the catalyst. In 1910, the Mann-Elkins Act turned the tables on the railroads and began to swing the power dynamics firmly toward the federal government for the first time. The Mann-Elkins Act had three main components; first, the ICC could now initiate proceedings against railroad rates directly. In the past, the ICC had to receive a complaint from a customer who felt they had been injured; now the ICC could go after the railroads themselves. Second, the act brought new strength to the prohibitions against short- and long-haul discrimination, especially in passenger traffic. Lastly, the act provided for a court to hear complaints between the ICC and the various railroads; however, this court was quickly dissolved by Congress after throwing out 90 percent of the complaints against railroads they heard.

The Mann-Elkins Act's most important provision, however, may well have been placing the burden of proof for rate increases on the railroads themselves. Previously, the ICC was required, after having a complaint brought to them, to prove the rate was unjust. Now the railroads needed to prove any rate they published was *just*. While this was seemingly a minor change in wording, the railroads' ability to adapt to changing economic times was now severely limited, and the ICC had gained the upper hand in most rate disputes. When coupled with the strengthened portion of the act that allowed the ICC to set rates, "the commission is hereby authorized [by this Act] and empowered to determine and prescribe what will be the just and reasonable individual or joint rate," leaving no question about Congress's intent this time that the ICC was firmly in control of railroad rates.

The response from the railroads was intense. It was clear to many that this act, to go into effect at the end of 1910, was going to place them under severe restrictions. This was coupled with a period of high inflation that, according to the St. Louis Fed, had been ongoing since the late 1890s. With these new restrictions, the railroads would be at a distinct disadvantage when it came to adjusting rates to the wildly fluctuating economy of the late nineteenth and early twentieth centuries. One article from October 1910 in the *Morning Journal* (Lancaster, Pennsylvania) noted a summit of "100 Railroad Lawyers" who were meeting at the Astoria hotel in New York to find any flaws or loopholes within the act before it was to go into effect. As usual, the Granger Roads were deeply involved, and one of the men reportedly at the Astoria meeting was J.J. Hill, president of the Great Northern and by extension the CB&Q. However, public opinion seems to have been favorable, with reports such as this one in the *Billings Evening Journal*:

> *As a whole the new law may be regarded as a distinct step toward the wider federal regulation and control of corporations against which radical state's rights advocates inveigh but which many thoughtful students of political economy believe necessary for the protection of the public.*

It seemed then that the pendulum of regulation had again swung firmly back in favor of the people and the government, and there was little that the railroads could do to fight back this time. The Progressives, led prominently by Theodore Roosevelt and later William Taft, had repaired all that ailed the original Interstate Commerce Act and arguably strengthened the position of the ICC in the face of powerful enemies in the rail industry. The great dream of the Grangers had been achieved and the people were no longer subservient to the railroads, but this presents the question, Were the Progressive Era reforms effective?

One method by which to investigate the railroads' relative health was miles built. In the Progressive Era, combined railroad construction reached its overall peak in 1902 with just over 6,000 miles. In only one year since has there been any more than 4,500 miles built. The obvious issue with looking at mileage added was that by the early twentieth century, the nation was saturated with rail. By 1910, the United States contained 351,000 miles of rail, and the network reached its overall peak in 1916 just prior to U.S. entry into World War I.

Perhaps a better indicator would be to investigate the profitability of the various Granger Roads to see if the railroad barons were indeed now at the behest of the federal government. Starting with the Milwaukee Road (CM&StP), we can read in their 1910 annual report a net revenue of $20.955 million on roughly $64 million in gross revenue. In 1916, the Milwaukee Road reported a net revenue of $36.525 million on roughly $105 million in gross revenue. While the costs were increasing and the revenue-to-cost ratio was getting smaller, the Milwaukee Road was still making significant profits throughout the Progressive Era's most stringent regulations.

While full data is hard to come by for the Progressive years, we can use documents like the Iowa Railroad Commission's reports to get a snapshot of the financial health of the Granger lines that operated in the state. The CB&Q had a listed full line revenue of $87.869 million in the 1910 report and expenses totaling $63.010 million for a total net profit of $24.859 million, while the 1916 report shows a total line expense of $61.713 million. Still, revenues rose to $100.280 million, giving a net profit of $38.567 million. The Rock Island route saw a revenue of $62.232 million and overall expenses of $45.474 million for a total net positive of $16.758 million in 1910 but an even better margin in 1916 with total operating revenues of $72.189 million and expenses of only $17.600 million for a total of $54.589 million in income. Lastly, the Chicago and North Western's numbers in the report match up closely with its fellow Grangers in the Iowa reports, showing a total net positive of $12.693 million in 1910 and $29.361 million in 1916.

With a wide view, we can see that when purely looking at the height of the Progressive Era, during the most restrictive years of the ICC to this point, the railroads, while publicly voicing their frustration and holding meetings to find any flaws in the new legislation, were still doing well.

Their margins may have been narrowing somewhat, but that argument would have hardly held any weight with the Grangers or more modern Progressives and may have even served to encourage further action, as curbing the excesses of the railroads was exactly what they had set out to do in the 1870s. In receiving its newfound powers during the Progressive Era, the ICC set the standard for many of the future bureaucracies that would come to characterize the modern regulatory system of the U.S. government, where more and more of the work of regulating various industries was taken away from the legislators directly and granted to regulatory bodies set up by legislation. However, the ICC's regulations also slowed the process of change, leaving the burden on the railroads to prove price changes were warranted and severely limiting their ability to respond to economic conditions quickly.

As the 1910s pushed on, more issues were dumped into the ICC's lap, including a 1916 rail strike. During a tense period when the United States was officially neutral but also doing its best to prepare for war should it arrive from the distant shores of Europe (where World War I had been raging for two years), the Railroad Brotherhood Union was agitating for an eight-hour workday and the railroad management was standing firm. Congress, pressured by President Woodrow Wilson, blinked first, passing the Adamson Act, which legally obligated the railroads to honor the eight-hour day, but not before many in the United States advocated further enhancing the ICC and granting it the power to arbitrate labor disputes as well. One article from the *Lake Geneva Herald* of Wisconsin said, "The public will not long maintain the role of innocent bystander. The Interstate Commerce Commission should be empowered to prevent this threatened railroad strike. Congress can so empower it." However, an even greater affront to the Granger railroads' power was coming, one that had been whispered about and discussed for as far back as the Omaha Platform, and it came not from the ICC or even Congress but from the president himself.

In 1916, with war on the horizon, Congress passed the Army Appropriations Act, which outlined in broad strokes the options available to the president in times of war when it came to transportation systems within the United States. The United States joined World War I with a declaration of war on April 6, 1917. By December, Wilson, desperately trying to mobilize a nation unprepared for war, had taken action, and on December 28, the U.S. government took control of the railroads of the nation. With the air of nationalism and cooperative action, by many accounts, the event was seen as a positive step. The *Rock Island Argus* reported on December 2, "The members of the war board—all railroad executives…pledged their support to the government administration as has practically every railroad man in the country." Within the same paper, beyond the practical and material benefits of having all railroads working together under unified management, the greater idea of public management of utilities was still being praised: "Under President Wilson's decision the great event, regarded by many as the opening of a new epoch in government operation and control of public utilities, passed by without any formal ceremony." Likewise, the *La Crosse Tribune* reported that "Mr. Garretson also added that the brotherhoods were all behind the government operation plan, and the president had known it for two weeks."

Under this plan, the competition, seen as vital to the economic health of the nation in peacetime, was eliminated. This ironically created a single government-controlled monopoly to streamline freight movement across the nation and eliminate unnecessary routes and passenger travel to free up more cars and locomotives to move war goods around the nation and to the ports of departure for Europe. However, those dreaming—as the previous articles noted—for a "new epoch" would be disappointed. In 1918, Congress passed the Railroad Control Act, guaranteeing the return of the railroads to private ownership within twenty-one months of the conclusion of peace. Perhaps most importantly, the law provided for the "just compensation" of roads that had been nationalized. This compensation was calculated as the average yearly income the roads had received from 1914 to 1917, prorated for the term that the railroad was held under federal control plus allowances for expansion, maintenance and repairs incurred during federalization. This act also placed the ICC in charge of any reimbursement claims, in cases where a railroad felt it was entitled to more compensation than was being offered.

When viewed as a whole, the Progressive Era seemed to be the crowning achievement of nearly forty years of popular action against the perceived abuses of the railroads against their clientele. The fight that began in the 1870s with the Granger Acts in Illinois, Iowa, Wisconsin and Minnesota had culminated with the ICC, a near copy-paste of those early state laws. However, the ICC had been neutered by Congress but was then revived through court action and renewed legislative action in the first decade of the twentieth century. As World War I brought even further regulation and government control, the roads had no choice but to give in. Yet, as the data shows, this in no way meant that the Granger Roads were suffering. In fact, they were growing right up to the government-imposed restrictions of the war years. Despite challenges from new technology, the Granger Roads emerged from the 1910s as strong as ever and looking toward a new dawn after being restored to private control. The 1920s were ahead, and the U.S. economy looked poised for a boom, supplying a war-shattered Europe. Yet the ever-present specter of an economic crash loomed. The railroads had persevered before, but the next panic would be unlike anything they had seen yet.

6

THE GREAT DEPRESSION AND THE END OF RAILROAD MONOPOLY

The 1920s were a period of intense change in the United States. An economic boom increased incomes for millions of Americans, and changes in labor laws allowed those same citizens to use their new-found income to pursue myriad leisure activities. According to the Gilder Lehrman Institute, incomes nearly doubled in the five years between 1919 and 1924 alone, while the cost of automobiles dropped by nearly half. This change led to a massive boom in automobile ownership among U.S. citizens. By 1929, over twenty-three million cars were roaming the developing network of roads and highways, almost four times as many as at the beginning of the decade.

The changes didn't end there. Census data shows that in 1920, for the first time in U.S. history, more people lived in urban areas than rural areas. This meant fewer and fewer people living in the many far-flung towns that had grown up along the railroad routes, especially across the Midwest, where farming towns made up many of the intermediate stops on the Granger railroads. The effect was seen throughout the 1920s; passengers carried by the railroads peaked at 1,269,918 in 1920 according to census data and fell to 786,432 by 1929, a drop of 38 percent within a single decade. At the same time ridership was falling, railroads were consolidating at an accelerating rate. While the number of Class I and II railroads operating in the United States remained relatively consistent through the 1910s, ending in 1919 with 1,111, by 1929 the number was down to 809. We can safely assume that this change was due to

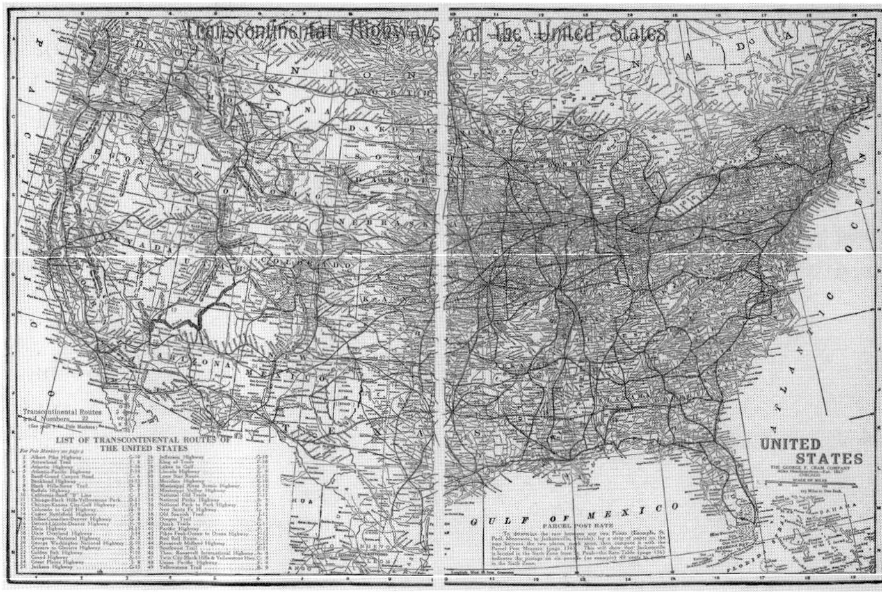

Transcontinental Highway Map, 1920. *David Rumsey Map Archive.*

consolidation, as the number of railroad miles in operation remained, within a small margin, essentially flat through the same period.

However, the economy was still booming, and freight tonnage generally rose throughout the decade, beginning at around 413 billion tons carried at least one mile and peaking at 450 billion tons carried at least one mile in 1929. The railroads were already beginning to exhibit a slow move from primarily passenger-driven services to freight. This had always been a key component of their business, especially in the Midwest, where farm products drove much of the growth, but no longer were trains the only viable method to move people quickly from point A to point B. The railroad companies were seeing this transition happen throughout the decade.

This passenger transition can be brought into further focus by looking at the estimated vehicle miles traveled in the United States during this time. According to the Federal Highway Administration in 1920, Americans drove 47.6 million miles on just over 3 million miles of public road. However, by 1929, that number had soared to 197.7 million miles on 3.2 million miles of public road. The car was transforming the lives of Americans, and what had once been a novelty during the Progressive Era was now a full-fledged competitor with the railroads. However, little was changing at the Interstate Commerce Commission to allow the railroads to compete.

As if to add insult to injury, air travel was also beginning to find its feet. By late 1930, Eastern Air Transport, later renamed Eastern Airlines, was already linking cities across the Northern Hemisphere. In December 1930, the *Brooklyn Daily Times* reported that in 1931 Eastern Air Transport would add new lines across the country: "With the New Year the New York-Atlanta air passenger service will be extended to St. Petersburg and Miami, joining Florida with New York and California for the first time, by regular air services, and forging the last link in the chain of passenger services that extend from Canada to Chile and Uruguay, and from Boston and Miami to Los Angeles." This rapid extension of air networks was possible in large part due to the minimal infrastructure needed outside of the destination and departure points for airlines. Whereas railroads need infrastructure along the entire route of travel, airlines simply needed airports at intervals for refueling and at their destinations; furthermore, airlines shared space at airports rather than each needing independently owned infrastructure. However, railroads were limited to their own track or tracks they were leasing from other

Eastern Airlines DC-3 Aircraft, 1941. *Library of Congress.*

lines. In the same issue of the *Brooklyn Daily Times*, it was reported that airline travel was "Seen as Safe as Finest Railroad Trains." Air travel also saw rapid growth in terms of passengers served. According to the Smithsonian Air and Space Museum, ridership in 1929 was only around 6,000; however, in five years it rose to 450,000, even amid the throes of the Great Depression.

All of this meant that the railroads, limited in their ability to change rates without asking and often suing the ICC for permission, were stuck using rates that were competitive when they were the only mass transit option available but now competing with two new technologies. With more passenger competition from more flexible and less resource-intensive modes of transportation, the railroads were being squeezed and forced to rely further on their freight incomes, where they held an advantage in efficiency. All the while, the ICC was pushing for consolidation as a means of raising the efficiency of the American rail system. Beginning with the Transportation Act of 1920, Harvard economist William Ripley was tasked with creating a plan for consolidating the nation's railroads to ensure that the weak railroads holding much of the nation's mileage wouldn't fail and leave communities without rail connections. This report was finished by 1921 and, according to the *St. Louis Globe-Democrat*, was to consolidate the hundreds of systems down to just nineteen. However, this plan was immediately attacked, according to the article, by railroad executives and stockholders. Even amid this atmosphere of uncertainty and restriction from the ICC, the railroads were still in relative strength during the 1920s, held up by the strong economy, but all of that changed in the span of a few short years.

However, this competition between the various Granger Roads as well as competition from these new modes of travel began to wear on some of the railroads. The Milwaukee Road had expanded its network all the way to the Pacific between 1906 and 1909 with its Pacific Extension. This extension was by all accounts a marvel; in 1909, it was reported that the road had erected a record number of bridges along a section of the Musselshell River in Montana. Over 20 miles of trestles made up 115 crossings of the river in a 117-mile stretch. The *Kenney Gazette* reported that the Milwaukee Road had shortened the distance from Chicago to Seattle by up to 144 miles over competitor routes. The line extension was subsidized through a bond sale; in January 1909, the *La Crosse Tribune* reported that $200 million in bonds were to be sold to fund the undertaking.

The story of the Pacific Extension and its electrification is fascinating and told in great detail in William Middleton's book *When the Steam Railroads Electrified*, in which he pointed out two major details that concern the discussion here. First, he noted, "The original estimated cost of $60 million was exceeded by more than 300 percent." While this cost was laid out in the early 1900s during the heyday of American rail as a mode of transportation, the bonds that were sold to cover the cost needed to be paid, and it so happened that the maturity of those bonds occurred in the 1920s. He also noted that the electrification came later in the period immediately up to the First World War, stating, "The entire 438-mile electrification between Harlowton and Avery was completed by the end of 1916....The railroad's board of directors was delighted by the Montana electrification and on January 25th 1917, authorized a further 207 miles." This project made the Milwaukee Road the largest electrified railroad in the world at the time but also put the railroad in a precarious financial position.

The Milwaukee Road hung on through expansion and consolidation until 1925. In March 1925, the *Wilkes-Barre Times Leader* reported that rumors were circulating that the Milwaukee Road was to enter receivership. On March 18, the reports were confirmed in the *Brooklyn Daily Eagle*: "A receivership for the Chicago, Milwaukee, and St. Paul Railway was signed by Judge James A. Wilkerson in the United States District Court

Postcard advertising the Olympian Hiawatha service, 1914. *Wikimedia Commons (public domain).*

here today upon the application of the Binkley Coal Company of this city." The effects were immediate. The *Buffalo News* reported only three days later, "The bankruptcy of the Chicago, Milwaukee, and St. Paul, coupled as it was with the great fall in wheat prices which are now about 50 cents below the high point reached some two months ago, has brought uneasiness into the farm circles." While the railroad later emerged from its receivership in a plan agreed to in June and amended in November 1925, the failure shook the already fragile farm market and, in retrospect, was an indication of what was to come.

A farm depression had been ongoing since the mid-1920s, bearing an eerie resemblance to the events that pushed the railroads and farmers into their first major clashes in the 1870s. As the Civil War had driven demand, World War I had also increased crop demand in the United States to be sent to Europe. According to the USDA's report *Crop Production Historical Track Records* from April 2019, in the years between 1910 and 1930, corn production peaked in 1917 with 110,000 acres planted, but in 1919, that number dropped dramatically to 87,000 acres. Similarly, barley production peaked in 1918 with 9,000 acres planted but dropped nearly 33 percent to only 6,500 acres in 1919. The data is similar in

Photograph of George Segal's sculpture *Depression Bread Line*, in Washington, D.C. *Kevin Burkett via Creative Commons.*

many regards to other major food crops such as beans, a peak in the waning days of World War I only for production to rapidly subside as the nation returned to peacetime demand.

Yet there was another force at work in the 1910s and '20s that had also been a factor in the 1870s: mechanization. This time the issue was not horse-drawn implements but motorized tractors. As steam engines on farms began to lose market share to the gasoline engine, farmers could begin to replace their costly and slow draft animals with motorized tractors. Once again, Henry Ford was at the center of the industry with his Fordson tractor, but this time other forces more familiar to Great Plains farmers were at work as well, with McCormick and John Deere also fielding early attempts at mass-market tractors. According to data from the National Bureau of Economic Research's article "The Diffusion of the Tractor in American Agriculture: 1910–1960," in 1920 only 3.6 percent of farms nationwide reported having a tractor. This number was slightly higher in the "West North Central" and "East North Central" regions with 8.4 percent and 5.1 percent, respectively. However, by 1930, that number had jumped to 13.5 percent nationally, 26.5 percent in the West North Central and 24.7 percent in the East North Central. This outlay of capital was not cheap, but it did have a purpose: to make cultivating larger areas of land more labor effective and to put more crops into production. The problem was that farm prices had been falling throughout the decade. According to the St. Louis Fed, the crop price index fell from a high of 290 in 1920 to as low as 114 in 1926, wiping out more than half the value of the crops. The index stabilized until 1930, when it plummeted further as the Great Depression began in earnest. In the end, the farmers were forced to accept lower prices with stable shipping rates while under the pressure of huge debt to mechanize, which had the knock-on effect of continuing to depress prices.

October 24, 1929, Black Thursday, is often cited as day 0 of the Great Depression, America's worst financial crisis. Historians have long debated the causes of the Depression, with high tariffs around the world, over-speculation on the stock market and poor banking regulation often cited as the most likely causes. What is not debated is the effect on the economy of the United States. According to the FDR Presidential Library, by 1933, 24.9 percent of the workforce was unemployed, and a farm depression that began in the 1920s further exacerbated the issue.

Despite the chaos besetting the farming industry in the 1920s, it was the series of events begun by the stock market panic in October 1929 that pushed the United States—and by extension many of the nation's industrialized economies—into a depression only fully resolved by the outbreak of World War II. Much has been written and is still debated about the root causes of the Great Depression, but among the most commonly cited issues were over-reliance on credit for consumers, which created a net negative savings rate; rampant stock market speculation; and banking regulations that were too weak to prevent bank failures when the panic truly took off in 1930 and into 1931.

According to the National Bureau of Economic Research, by the fall of 1930, thirty-nine banks were failing per week across the nation. Members of those banks ran to pull out any funds that were left, and banks with low reserves couldn't handle the sudden demand for money. In all, according to the NBER, across the nation, the money supply dipped by over 30 percent in the first years of the depression. As a result, many families had their savings wiped out, many investors were left destitute and the cost of doing business during a time of deflation increased dramatically. Industries that required large amounts of capital to do business, like railroads, found it hard if not impossible to find credit.

In the first two years of the Great Depression, the Hoover administration continued to rely heavily on private charity and good-faith discussions between industry and labor to try to alleviate the effects of the Depression. History, and indeed those contemporary to Hoover, have not been kind to his administration's handling of the affair. One only need look to the Bonus Army or the fact that in many locales the shanty towns popping up to house those who had lost homes were dubbed "Hoovervilles." Nevertheless, by the end of his term, Hoover had begun to move toward more direct government action and formed the Reconstruction Finance Corporation.

The purpose of the RFC was to provide government-secured loans to companies within certain vital industries to prevent their failure. According to the RFC's final report in 1959, upon signing the bill for its creation, Hoover is quoted as having said,

> *It brings into being a powerful organization with adequate resources, able to strengthen weaknesses that may develop in our credit, banking and railway structure, in order to permit business and industry to carry on normal activities free from the fear of unexpected shocks and retarding influences.*

Thus, we can see that the nation still regarded rail transport as one of the most important industries during the Great Depression. However, according to an article written for the Center for Economic and Policy Research, no link can be found to railways that received RFC loans and their long-term health, nor their ability to keep or raise employment.

In the lead-up to the Great Depression and during the first two years, the ICC also played an outsized role, as it had since the Progressive Era. The Esch-Cummins Act, more popularly known as the Transportation Act of 1920, raised rates for freight after returning railroads to private ownership after World War I, and those rates had stayed high throughout the 1920s, in effect raising the cost of shipment. According to an article by Paul Sharp and Giovanni Federico, throughout the 1920s, the ICC was happy to keep the status quo, rejecting the railroad's requests for rate hikes and shippers' requests for rate drops.

According to the same article, as farm prices plummeted in the first years of the Depression, the ICC held fast to its rates, even as railroad owners asked for a 15 percent increase. This drop in prices when compared to a steady rate of shipment meant that the cost of shipping ate further into the earnings of farmers and businesses, further exacerbating the issue. Even as traffic reached 40 percent of its 1929 level in 1932, the ICC had yet to move its rates at all. It was not until 1934 that the ICC moved the shipping rates, and then only a 10 percent reduction, citing the perilous state of railroad companies during the time as the reasoning for their reluctance to make any moves prior to that point. In the end, it appears, as Frederico and Sharp asserted, that the ICC during the Great Depression did a great service to railroads "at the expense of consumers and the whole American economy paid a price."

Still, despite the best efforts of the ICC and the RFC before it, railroads suffered. According to the Association of American of Railroads, in the first four years of the Depression, revenues fell by 50 percent, and by 1937, seventy thousand miles of rail within the nation were in receivership. The railroads also took on a new challenge: the hobo riding the rails came to be synonymous with the Depression. Railroads often hired rail police to prevent freeloading and property damage from the scores of men who struck out across the country hoping to use a passing freight train as an easy ticket out of their current situation. The Granger Roads had faced adversity and come out on top before, and the Great Depression was no different.

Despite the challenges facing the Granger Roads in the 1920s and into the Great Depression, many of the roads continued to prosper. Many cite the 1920s and '30s as the golden age of rail travel. As the railroads saw competition for their riders for the first time in history, this competition drove a sharp rise in not only the comfort and relative opulence of rail travel but also safety. The rail corridors between Chicago and St. Paul as well as to and from the West became the scene of new services promising comfort and speed never seen before in American rail service and, in some cases, services around the globe.

The first road to debut a new groundbreaking service was the CB&Q with its Zephyr. The Burlington and Quincy co-opted a new technology of their own to fight against the rising tide of airlines and car travel, the diesel-electric locomotive. Debuting in 1934, the Zephyr featured a highly streamlined body, new diesel-electric engines and a PR campaign that included a western tour and Hollywood movie. In fact, according to Richard C. Overton's *Burlington Route: A History of the Burlington Lines*, the Zephyr was the very first streamlined diesel-electric train set to be used in the United States. The Zephyr reportedly made a nonstop trip from Denver to Chicago, reaching speeds in excess of 110 miles per hour, while only costing the railroad $14.64 in fuel. A new dawn had arrived in railroading, but one that would be costly. Previous locomotive technology had been evolutionary, and railroads could simply phase out old steam locomotives as new ones came onto the lines, but with the diesel-electrics, there was the possibility that much of the railroad infrastructure—water towers, coaling stations, steam works and more—was going to be obsolete and new fleets of locomotives would be needed, an extreme outlay during the dark days of the Great Depression.

However, it was the Twin Cities Zephyr that drove competition and raised the bar among the various Granger Roads. Covering the journey from Chicago and St. Paul in around five and a half hours at an average speed of seventy-seven miles per hour, the CB&Q had set a new standard for the busy and competitive route. The other Granger Roads were going to need to respond or risk losing valuable passenger revenue at a time when the ICC was reluctant to raise freight rates. In 1932, the ICC had allowed some increases, but times were tight among the many railroads and bankruptcy was always just around the corner.

In 1934, the CNW began preparations for its own high-speed passenger service. According to Roger Grant's *The North Wester: A History of the Chicago and North Western Railway System*, the CNW was worried about the CB&Q's rumored new streamliners and began discussions on how to counter the threat. The railway quickly created a new route dubbed the Adams Cutoff to skip some of the high grades in western Wisconsin, reshaped curves and did everything it could to get its "400" Train service ready. The route was so named because the planned service would take 400 minutes to cover 400 miles between the two major cities, an average of 60 miles per hour, including limited stops. Unlike the CB&Q, the CNW saved money and skipped buying new diesel-electrics and instead used steam power to drive the new services using oil-fired Pacific-class locomotives. By January 1935, the 400 was shuttling some ten thousand passengers per month quickly and comfortably between Chicago and St. Paul and saved money in the process.

Not wanting to miss out, the Milwaukee Road introduced its high-speed passenger service in 1935 as well, calling their train set the Hiawatha. Delayed somewhat from the CB&Q and the CNW, the Hiawatha made its maiden test run in May 1935 on a truncated route from Milwaukee to New Lisbon, Wisconsin. In *The Milwaukee Road: Its First 100 Years* August Derleth mentioned that passengers felt that the train seemed as comfortable at speeds nearing and over one hundred miles per hour as it did at forty-five miles per hour. The Milwaukee Road found the same success as the CB&Q and the CNW, finding that high-speed luxury rail, at least for the time being, was an antidote to the ever-increasing road travel that had so far been eroding the passenger numbers. The Milwaukee Road had also opted for steam-powered services with a streamlined shell, likely owing

Postcard advertising the CNW's 400 service. *Wikimedia Commons (public domain).*

Hiawatha Streamliner at the Milwaukee Road station in Milwaukee, Wisconsin. *Milwaukee Public Library, Milwaukee Road Archives.*

to the precarious financial position that the railroad had been in since its post-expansion reorganization.

The Rock Island would be somewhat delayed with the introduction of its streamlined service. Beginning in 1937, the CRI&P followed the lead of competitor CB&Q and introduced new diesel-electric streamliners called the "Rocket." Reports abound in period newspapers like the *Dayskin Herald*, in which reporters wrote of the trains running through Plymouth, Nebraska, at "over 70 miles per hour" and mentioned that "quite a number of people were on hand to see the trains pass through town." However, the introduction of the Rocket also highlighted the dangers of the railroads' rapid speed increases without appropriate safety measures in place. On October 22, 1937, it was reported that a Rock Island Rocket train hit a school bus while en route from Kansas City to Minneapolis in Mason City, Iowa. Reports from the *St. Louis Globe-Democrat* list ten killed and another eighteen injured; among the dead was the bus driver, an English teacher and eight children, while no one on the train was injured. The *Daily Nonpareil* reported on October 25 that it was the failure of the bus driver to properly heed crossing signals that was determined to be the cause of the accident and that the engineer of the train had no idea there was an imminent collision until "he saw bits of wood flying past his windshield."

Certainly, these new train services were a spectacle, both in the positive and negative senses of the word. The public was fascinated by a revolution in railroading happening right before their eyes yet also appalled at the consequences when things went wrong. However, despite the small reprieve the Granger Roads found through their new services, none fully escaped the effects of the Great Depression. The first line to stumble was the Rock Island, in June 1933. In the *Big Spring Daily Herald*, it was reported that the Rock was entering a reorganization after being unable to meet its financial liabilities. The CNW went bankrupt two years later in 1935 and took nine years to emerge from reorganization. The Milwaukee Road, ever in danger after its Pacific Extension, filed for bankruptcy in June 1935, a process that did not conclude until the waning days of World War II. The CB&Q was the lone Granger to stand tall throughout the Great Depression without filing for bankruptcy, but like the others it was still struggling under changing modes of transportation and hard economic times.

Streamlined diesel locomotive used for the Rock Island's "Rocket" service. *Wikimedia Commons (public domain).*

Where then was the ICC, whose mission it was to ensure the health of the nation's railroads and to balance that health with fair prices for passengers and shippers alike? As previously mentioned, the ICC waited until 1932 to adjust rates and only then cut shipping rates by 10 percent. Over following twelve years—which included World War II—the ICC adjusted rates only a further six times, and even then the rate adjustments were incremental and conservative. While a rising tide raises all boats, the inverse is also true, and the Great Depression decimated the railroads. According to U.S. Census data, in the twelve years between the stock market crash and the eve of World War II, the United States lost around 250 railroad operators. In that same period, rail mileage contracted heavily as well, with the nation losing 17,500 miles or around 7 percent of the total rail mileage in the United States in 1929. This was especially stark considering the relative stability of the rail network in the United States from 1916 to 1929.

Despite the best efforts of the RFC and the ICC, as well as the myriad "alphabet agencies" of the New Deal under Franklin Roosevelt, the railroads could not escape the heavy losses that all industries were taking. As the railroads were intrinsically linked to diverse industries, there was no surefire way to insulate themselves from the catastrophe that was the Great Depression. There were, however, some silver linings to be found. Despite many of the Granger Roads experiencing bankruptcy, many were also beginning to introduce new technologies and improved services to try to compete in the thinning passenger market, and none of the Granger Roads was among those unfortunate companies that failed completely during the Depression.

In 1941, the Granger Roads were again poised to take advantage of world events far beyond their control. Once again, the clouds of war were darkening on the horizon. Despite the neutrality acts of the 1930s, by 1941, the United States was fully engaged in the Lend-Lease program, leveraging manufacturing in the heartland to refit the British and later Soviet militaries fighting the Nazi war machine. According to census data, between 1938 and 1941 freight tonnage across the United States grew by over 450,000 tons as the United States began its transition to the "Arsenal of Democracy." According to annual reports, the Milwaukee Road posted a net deficit in 1939 of $14.4 million and $8.8 million in 1940; however by the end of 1941, they had posted a net surplus of $5.5 million. Likewise, the CB&Q posted a net surplus of $3.6 million in 1939, but by 1941 that number was $10.4 million. While data is missing for the Rock Island and the CNW for the same time frame, the lesson is clear. The war economy was good for the railroads, as it had been during World War I. However, the war and its requirements slowed the otherwise rapid pace of technological change.

In 1941, the steam locomotive was reaching its engineering pinnacle and the diesel-electric was still new and unproven. The War Productions Board even stepped in to put a development freeze on new locomotive designs, hoping to ensure less waste and more efficient production. Yet some of the most iconic steam locomotives produced were built during and immediately after the war, having received special dispensation from the WPB. The federal government once again stepped in to help coordinate the war effort on the rails, this time through the Office of Defense Transportation. So dire was the need for locomotives and railcars that production reached four thousand locomotives during the war, and there was even a temporary railcar shortage in 1939. Thanks to the renewed economic activity, funded nearly entirely by the U.S. government, rail freight revenues soared. According to census data, total freight revenues for Class I, II and III railroads in 1939 was around $3.3 billion, already up from a mere $2.4 billion in 1932. However, by 1945, the collective railroads were bringing in $6.6 billion in freight, doubling their revenues in the span of six years. The rapid turnaround was similar for passenger service. Census data shows an increase from around $417 million in 1939 to over $1.7 billion in 1945, a more than 400 percent increase over those six years. All of this business meant that those railroads that had entered bankruptcy during the Depression could exit the process near or shortly after the war ended. The *La Crosse Tribune* reported on November 27, 1945, that the Milwaukee Road's reorganization had been approved on the twenty-sixth and would be able to enter the postwar period anew. The Chicago and North Western got back on its feet somewhat earlier, as the *Chattanooga Daily Times* reported on June 4, 1944, that "The Chicago & North Western was among the last of the major railway systems to go down in the depression....It will be the first to assume a solvent status." The article further stated that as of June 1, all of the property had been returned after the approval of their reorganization plan. The Rock Island had to wait the longest of the Granger Roads for its reorganization plan to be approved. Finally, on January 5, 1948, *The M'Alester News-Capital* reported as of January 1, 1948, that the Rock had officially been dismissed from its receivership after many years of investigation and foot-dragging from the ICC.

Thus the Granger Roads, flush with cash and for the time on a strong financial footing, entered the middle decades of the twentieth century. It was becoming apparent that the undisputed reign of rail transport was over, and new waves of technology were beginning to drive costs. The question was no longer if the Granger Roads could capitalize; the question became could the Granger Roads simultaneously navigate the maze of red tape they had inadvertently helped create more than seventy-five years prior and adjust to the new economic landscape of a rapidly changing America?

7

DECLINE, DEREGULATION AND CONSOLIDATION

While World War II brought a temporary reprieve and, in the cases of the Granger Roads, a safety net to escape bankruptcy, the 1950s would see a rapid return to the issues that had slowly been eroding the dominance of the railroad in the first half of the twentieth century. In fact, the war both temporarily saved the railroads and accelerated their demise. The concept that "necessity is the mother of invention" perhaps found its roots in the golden age of the Greek philosophers, but it found its modern realization in World War II.

Automobiles had long been eroding railroad ridership; however, President Dwight D. Eisenhower, hero of Normandy, sent this movement into overdrive. As a young soldier back in 1919, Eisenhower had been a part of a cross-country military convoy. The trip from Washington, D.C., to San Francisco took sixty-two grueling days. This experience affected the man who would go on to lead Allied forces through Germany. His experiences while fighting the Axis led him to the Autobahn, and he realized the advantages of having a national system of high-speed highways to move citizens as well as war materials and fighting men around the nation's vast interior.

In 1954, Eisenhower signed a bill to increase federal funding for highways across the nation, to supercharge the efforts to provide high-quality paved roads to connect the various towns and cities of the United States. Within the bill was funding for an "Interstate Highway System" These new roads would connect the nation with multilane highways from East Coast to West and North to South like nothing the nation yet knew. This new phase of highway construction coincided with a postwar industrial boom that saw car production soar to heights never seen before, Chevrolet and Ford alone produced over twenty-five million cars during the decade, in a nation that was home to fewer than two hundred million citizens. Americans now had access to vehicles and the roads to take them quickly and comfortably wherever they wanted to go, as long as they were happy to take their time.

The effect of the federal highway funding was immense: according to census data, beginning in 1952, the federal highway system added over twenty thousand miles per year for over a decade, not dipping below that number until 1963. The same data shows the rapid decline in intercity travel by rail, as cars became the primary mode of transportation. By 1950, in terms of passenger miles, private cars made up 86 percent of all passenger miles, while railroads accounted for only 6.4 percent. However, by 1959, railroads account for only 2.9 percent, while cars were accounting for 89.9 percent. Freight totals show a similar decline, although, as mentioned in previous chapters, the railroads were already beginning to pivot to freight as their primary means of revenue. In 1946, the first year after the war, railroads accounted for 68 percent of the nation's ton-miles of freight moved. Yet by 1959, only 46 percent of freight ton-miles were being moved by the nation's railroads, their share being usurped by the growing numbers of semitrucks plying the nation's new highway system. In 1946, motor vehicles accounted for only 8.6 percent of all ton-miles, but by 1959, they were hauling 21.4 percent. The railroads were being assailed by the new roads on both passenger and freight revenue streams.

Even worse for the railroads, wartime technology also solved the issue of long-distance transportation during the 1950s. Long-range strategic bombing became a cornerstone of the Allied war effort in the European and Pacific theaters throughout World War II, and as a result, the resources and energy put into producing longer-ranged, more reliable and heavier lifting aircraft paid dividends. At the outbreak of war, the B-17C, the primary strategic bomber within the U.S. Army Airforce, had a combat range with bombs loaded of 2,400 miles with a top speed of 323 miles per hour at around 25,000 feet according to Peter Bowers's *Boeing Aircraft Since 1916*. These numbers by themselves would be fairly impressive had it not been for the rapid pace of aircraft development during the war. By 1945, the B-29 had become the preeminent long-range bomber of any Allied or Axis air force. The B-29 could travel faster, with a top

Highways like this one in the Lehigh Valley allowed the car to be the primary mode of transportation. *Wikimedia Commons (public domain).*

speed of 365 miles per hour at the same 25,000-foot altitude. However, the crew was comfortable in a pressurized cabin, unlike the B-17 crews, who faced frostbite and hypoxia if they didn't dress for the warmth or if their oxygen ran out. Additionally, the B-29 could carry eight times the payload more than twice the distance.

When the war was over, much of the work to create bombers was translated neatly into civil aviation. Airlines began to fly iconic designs with their origins in World War II combat aircraft. The Lockheed Constellation began going up against the civilian derivation of the Boeing-produced B-29 called the Stratocruiser and the omnipresent Douglas aircraft like the DC-4 and DC-6 series of aircraft. The Stratocruiser was able to ferry up to one hundred passengers over 4,000 miles cruising at 340 miles per hour high above the clouds in its pressurized cabin, all characteristics initially designed for its wartime use. Furthermore, the many military airfields that had popped up around the nation during the war were quickly converted to peacetime use, and many more began to be constructed as cities grew.

The aforementioned census data tells the same tale as the highways, but this time in the air. In 1950, airlines accounted for only 2 percent of all passenger miles, but by 1959, planes had overtaken railroads by carrying 4.3 percent. When it came to freight, the airlines were admittedly behind, but the railroads were already in dire straits attempting to compete with long-haul trucking.

The ICC, in the interim, had been doing what it could to keep railroads afloat, as well as beginning to administer the nation's other modes of mass transportation. In 1935, the ICC had begun to regulate intercity bus lines as well as trucking and was tasked with protecting the railroads and trucking companies from competing against one another. Nevertheless, the rather slow and cumbersome nature of the ICC continued to dog the commission into the '50s and '60s.

Many of the railroads had seen precipitous drop-offs in passenger services, as mentioned earlier in the chapter. This lost revenue, while partially made up for with freight revenues, began to eat away at an industry that by the 1950s was dangerously bloated from a century of expansion. The commission was also slow to allow railroads to abandon failing routes, meaning that railroads were left holding onto unprofitable routes, further draining their resources. The 1950s, according to U.S. Census data, saw the beginning of a slow but steady decline in railroad mileage that peaked in the 1970s and '80s with the era of deregulation. In the early phases, beginning in 1950, the nation lost between five and

United Airlines Douglas DC-4 common in the postwar era. *Bill Larkins via Creative Commons, https://creativecommons.org/licenses/by-sa/2.0/.*

seven hundred miles of rail annually to abandonment, but the more startling loss was in passenger road mileage.

In the 1970 *Historical Statistics of the United States* from the Census Bureau, railroad miles dedicated to passenger use are detailed, beginning in the year 1936, when it was reported that, for Class I railroads, 178,000 miles of road were in use for passenger service, of the total 240,000 miles of road owned. By 1950, the number had fallen to 146,000 and further to 119,000 by 1955 and was under 100,000 by the first year of the following decade when it hit 93,000 in 1960. This 47 percent reduction in passenger miles stands in further contrast to the only 9.5 percent decline in overall road miles owned by Class I railroads during the same period. Clearly, the passenger service of the major railroads of the United States was becoming an unprofitable burden to these roads.

The ICC had historically been the greatest barrier to the railroads' flexibility in responding to market conditions. The ICC had been created with the Populist and Granger ideals that the railroads were out to harm the consumer, and as such, the power in decision-making should ultimately reside with the government. It was up to the railroads to prove any movement away from the newly created status quo. The ICC had upheld such injurious practices as an Ohio law that required railroads to stop at least three times daily at towns above certain population thresholds and a similar law that required local trains to stop at certain towns in Minnesota. However, the ICC did begin to see the writing on the wall, and Congress passed the Transportation Act of 1958 to attempt to stem some of the worst of the bleeding.

The 1958 act provided $500 million to the commission to loan to various railroads to make improvements and obtain capital. The act also provided a framework for the abandonment of passenger services in a new section 13A under section 5 of the act. In essence, the railroads were required to post a notice within thirty days of the change or end of a service, and if the ICC determined that the route was necessary, the railroad could be compelled by the commission to continue the service for up to another year. Another shot to the railroads was the change in the wording of section 6, which no longer protected modes of transportation against competing against one another but simply said that the commission would act to see whether rates were lower than reasonable without consideration of the competition between modes of transport.

As the railroads fought the ICC and the cumbersome bureaucratic red tape that had been wrapped so tightly around their industry by the legislative legacy of the Grangers, another force was weighing heavily on them—technological progress. One of the greatest changes to hit the railroads since their inception came with the move from steam to diesel-electric locomotives. Entire infrastructures built to sustain steam locomotives and their maintenance were becoming obsolete, and new locomotives needed to be bought to replace the aging and inefficient steam behemoths of the early twentieth century. The CB&Q had proven with their Zephyr train sets that diesel had a place on mainline railroads as early as the mid-1930s, but it was the introduction of the EMD E and F units alongside the Alco PA series through the 1940s and 1950s that began to rapidly escalate the changeover to diesel as they proved their reliability, strength and cost-effectiveness. It was estimated, by the American Association of Railroads, that by the mid-1950s, most railroads had shifted the majority of their motive power to diesel. However, steam hung on in Class I railroads until the early 1960s and even longer on some smaller routes.

As the 1950s pushed into the 1960s and '70s, it was clear that the railroads of the United States were struggling, and the current regulatory system, in place for nearly a century, was no longer sufficient to ensure their success or even survival. Something needed to be done. Many of the famous services of the Granger Roads were falling by the wayside as well, leaving their names to be found only in the history books.

The CNW's 400 train met its demise in 1961 when the CNW petitioned the ICC for the right to suspend the famous service. In an October 1961 article from the *Daily Telegram* of Eau Claire, Wisconsin, the railroad reported it was losing $6,400 a day running the Rochester and Twin Cities 400s. The loss

Postcard featuring a new diesel E-7 locomotive of the Great Northern Railroad. *Wikimedia Commons (public domain).*

An EMD SD45 diesel locomotive of Northern Pacific, common among Class I railroads during the 1960s and '70s. *Photo Credit: Craig Garver/Public Domain.*

was more than simply outdated equipment, as the 400s had been running on diesel power for some time. In the same article, the railroad noted a 22 percent drop on the Twin Cities route and 31 percent on the Rochester route. The railroad pointed out the overabundance of transportation between the Twin Cities and Chicago, as there were reportedly nineteen passenger services between the two destinations daily in 1961, in addition to bus and airline flights.

The Rock Island shut down its famous Rocky Mountain Rocket route in 1966 after nearly twenty-seven years of service. The various Milwaukee Road Hiawathas were shortened or outright discontinued through the 1950s. The Olympian Hiawatha hung on as late as 1961, when the Milwaukee Road petitioned the ICC for its demise as well. The *La Crosse Tribune* reported in February 1961 that the railroad was losing over $2 million a year running the route. The CB&Q's Zephyr, the train that started it all, hung on until 1971, when, along with all other passenger services run by Class I railroads, they ceased operation and handed off all passenger services to the new and only passenger operator from then on, Amtrak.

The Granger Roads were, as the 1960s turned to the '70s, back to almost where they had found themselves one hundred years earlier, serving primarily industry and agriculture. The 1968 Milwaukee Road Annual Report indicates freight revenues of $236.7 million, while passenger revenue accounted for only $19.6 million. Likewise, the CB&Q 1968 report showed $247.2 million in freight revenue and only $11.4 million in passenger revenues, and the CB&Q report noted a sharp 30 percent drop in grain traffic, making their freight revenue even more impressive. In the report, it is noted that freight accounted for eighty-six cents of every dollar earned by the CB&Q while passenger service accounted for only five cents. The story, while annual reports are missing for the same year, was the same for the Rock Island and CNW Railroads.

Times were so dire that by 1968 every one of the Granger railroads was in discussions with at least one other railroad about consolidation. The Milwaukee Road and CNW were engaged in negotiations with the ICC, the Rock was looking at joining the Union Pacific System and the CB&Q and Great Northern were looking to fully consolidate their decades-long informal relationship.

In the end, the CNW and Milwaukee Road merger was abandoned in 1970. In the *Belvidere Daily Republican* in April 1970, it was reported that the two railroads successfully applied for a cancelation of the merger from the ICC, which was approved on the grounds that they were unable to reach an agreement on stock exchange ratios. Such was the control of the ICC by 1970, nearing its one hundredth birthday, railways could neither enter nor break off merger negotiations without approval by the commission. Meanwhile, in the same year, the CB&Q ceased to exist, as it merged with the Great Northern, Northern Pacific and Spokane, Portland & Seattle Railroads to form the Burlington Northern Railway. In a full-page *Amarillo Globe-Times* advertisement in March 1970, the new railroad boasted that it now held twenty-five thousand miles of track reaching eighteen states and into Canada. The CB&Q thus became the first of the Grangers to fall, almost a perfect century after setting into motion the series of events that would lead to its own demise.

The Rock Island and Union Pacific merger failed to come to fruition in 1975. According to reporting in the *Daily Mail* on March 19, 1975, after receiving initial approval from the ICC, the Union Pacific had second thoughts on absorbing the financial disaster that the Rock had become. This left the Rock to attempt to reorganize itself in the ensuing years, now on its own in an industry where the once great Grangers were quickly becoming extinct.

However, at the same time as the Grangers evaluated their consolidation options, a seismic change was occurring in the halls of Washington, D.C. In October 1970, Congress passed and sent along to President Nixon the

A Milwaukee Road EMD E7 arrives in Milwaukee in 1963. *Photo credit: Rich Pinnisi.*

Rail Passenger Service Act, which he promptly signed. This act took the Populist dream of having the federal government run the rail network and made it a reality. The act took all passenger rail services within the United States and created a corporation called the National Passenger Rail Corporation, which ran under the name Amtrak as of 1971. The railroads that operated intercity services could voluntarily hand over their services effective May 1, 1971, and be freed from the obligations under the previous ICC rules to petition for their cancellation. In the act, Congress noted "that modern, efficient, intercity railroad passenger service is a necessary part of a balanced transportation system" and "travelers in America should to the maximum extent feasible have the freedom to choose the mode of travel most convenient to his needs." In essence, Congress understood the value of rail travel for passengers and that in the modern economic landscape it would need to be run as a public good rather than private venture.

The service was embattled but took the reins on May 1, 1971. According to reports in the *San Bernardino County Sun*, the service eliminated nearly two hundred trains across the nation, hoping to streamline their services

Passengers board the Southwest Limited service run by recently founded Amtrak in 1974. *United States National Archives.*

in an effort to make it profitable. The same paper noted that on the last day of private service, many trains leaving California were operating at nearly twice the load as both young and old attempted to ride some of the region's most famous trains one last time before the nationalization of the routes meant these trains would be discontinued. As it grew, Amtrak slowly moved from a collection of coaches and locomotives borrowed and inherited from the previous railroad operators to cars and locomotives entirely built and designed for the company.

The railroads were now free of their costly, inefficient and often burdensome passenger services, freed from having to make their case to the ICC for their discontinuation, and could focus on their freight services. Yet as the Granger Roads fought to stay afloat throughout the decade, an even more monumental decision from Capitol Hill was coming in 1980: rail deregulation.

Throughout the 1970s, multiple rail lines faced bankruptcy. In 1975, the Rock Island filed for the last time, a process that wouldn't conclude until 1980, when the *Belleville Telescope* reported that at the conclusion of bankruptcy proceedings, the railroad had amassed some $400 million in debt with little assets to show for it. The Milwaukee Road filed in 1977, a process not to be completed for another eight years. However, it was reported by the *Chillicothe Constitution-Tribune* in 1977 that a combination of droughts and future economic forecasts meant that the grain and lumber shipments the railroad depended on to stay solvent were no longer covering their liabilities.

However, perhaps the largest domino to fall in the 1970s was not a Granger but an East Coast giant, the Penn Central. Formed as a merger of the New York Central and Pennsylvania Railroad, the Penn Central was one of the nation's largest corporations, and its failure sent shockwaves through all sectors of the economy. Stockbrokers, congressmen, railroad men and shippers were all left to wonder, "If even the Penn Central could fall, who else was next?" In the end, the government stepped in and created the Consolidated Rail Corporation in 1976. Following a similar path as Amtrak, a government-subsidized railway was to take over the services of the former Penn Central to ensure that the industries served by the railroad would not fall as further dominoes and prevent a cascade effect across other industries.

The failure of so many large railroads in the 1970s raised the question, With such a stringent set of railroad regulations in place, was the time right to reevaluate the ICC and its iron grasp over the rails? The question was

A Milwaukee Road F unit is slowly pulling out of Madison, Wisconsin, with the state capital in the background. *Photo Credit: Mark Llanuza.*

answered in 1980 by the passage of the Staggers Act, which in essence ended the ninety-three-year reign of the ICC as the watchdog over the railroad corporations of the United States. A process begun in the fading light of Reconstruction ended in the twilight of the postwar economic boom.

The Staggers Act of 1980 was a watershed moment for the railroads. It was clear by this point that the shippers and citizens of the United States were no longer under the yoke of the railroads as they had been in the 1870s, and as such, their strict regulation was no longer needed. The act removed the ICC's jurisdiction for setting rates, except in areas where competition was absent, as the railroads could still theoretically set unfair rates in those scenarios. The act also removed prohibitions on shipping contracts, allowing individual companies to create contracts to negotiate their own rates directly with the railroads. The act further eased restrictions on mergers and consolidations, stating that the ICC "shall" approve these unless it could be proven that it would create a monopoly or that the anticompetitive effects of such a merger outweighed the potential benefit to the public. The process for abandoning rail lines was streamlined as well. For the railroads, this was a breath of fresh air; they were finally allowed the flexibility to move with the markets rather than fight against bureaucracy to stay alive.

The effects were immediate and impressive, according to a report from the Government Accountability Office. The rate of returns for railroad investment jumped from 2.5 percent in the '70s to 4.9 percent during the 1980s. The Federal Rail Administration also noted in their analysis of the act that since the act was implemented, inflation-adjusted shipping rates had consistently fallen by around .5 percent annually since the act, as opposed to a nearly 3 percent increase previous to its passage. The FRA also noted that increased financial stability had led to increases in infrastructure investment as well as safety increases since its passage. However, perhaps the most important statistic noted by the FRA in their report is that the railroad market share for freight, which had been steadily declining through the 1960s and '70s had stabilized in the years following the act's passage at around 40 percent.

It is remarkable that in such a short time, roughly from 1980 to 1988, the deregulation of the railroads had such a profound effect on their fortunes. That isn't to say, however, that the Grangers would all live to see this bright future, at least not in their original forms. As previously mentioned, the CB&Q had already consolidated into BN by the 1980s, and the other Grangers followed suit in short order.

As reported in the *Logansport Pharos-Tribune*, the Rock's five-year journey through bankruptcy ended on March 23, 1980, when the railroad ceased accepting new shipments and within weeks began to abandon lines and liquidate property. The 130-year-old icon of the Midwest died with a whimper, unable to consummate its deal with UP and simply rotting away, a victim of poor maintenance due to a lack of funds. The paper reported that in very short order, more than 2,400 workers were out of a job, and a full two-thirds of the railway's lines were abandoned, the other third being taken up by other railroad companies, including intracity services between Joliet and Chicago run by the CNW.

The Milwaukee Road also entered bankruptcy in the late 1970s, and according to reporting from February 1980 in the *Daily American Republic*, a plan had been approved to shrink the railroad to a more manageable size. The article stated that the Milwaukee Road would drop most of its Pacific extension; in all, around six thousand miles were trimmed from the railroad to attempt to reduce its size to just over three thousand miles and make it more efficient. However, despite the Milwaukie Road seeming to turn its fortunes around in the early years of the 1980s, by 1985, it had become clear that the reorganization was not going to end well and that the railroad would need to be purchased outright. On February 8, 1985, the *Chillicothe Constitution-Tribune* reported that the judge in the reorganization case had accepted the Soo Line's $570 million offer to purchase the remains of the once great Granger railroad and absorb it into the Soo Line system. Thus, after eight painful years, the final valiant effort of the Milwaukee Road was for naught and the third of the Grangers had fallen. The Soo Line spun off the former Wisconsin rail lines of the Milwaukee Road into the Wisconsin Central Railroad in the late 1980s. This regional railroad, the nation's largest at the time, was bought up by Canadian National in 2001, bringing the Milwaukee Road lines into a mega railroad in the twenty-first century.

And then there was one. By 1985, the only remaining Granger Road, at least in its original form, was the CNW. Despite numerous corporate restructurings, none requiring bankruptcy, the CNW continued on throughout the 1980s and into the early 1990s, but by 1994, the era of consolidation was fully underway and regional Class I railroads were quickly becoming extinct. According to the USDA, in 1980 there were thirty-three Class I railroads at the time the Staggers Act was passed, but by 1995, that number had dropped to eleven. It was only a matter of time until the CNW was snapped up by one of the increasingly large mega-railroads of the early 1990s.

Indeed, in March 1995, the *Kokomo Tribune* reported that the Union Pacific and CNW had reached an agreement amounting to around $1.6 billion. The UP would absorb the rest of the shares that they didn't already own in the CNW and fully absorb the last Granger into the rapidly expanding UP system. Later in the same year, the Burlington Northern, the spiritual successor to the CB&Q, snapped up the Santa Fe in a consolidation, reported in the *San Bernardino County Sun* to be a deal worth over $4 billion at the time and amounting to a network of over thirty-three thousand miles. In 1995, the UP went on to purchase the Southern Pacific as well, hoping to keep pace with the newly renamed Burlington Northern Sante Fe (BNSF) Railroad.

While other Class I roads did absorb and operate the former Granger rail lines, many local lines looked as if they would be abandoned had other smaller short-line railroads not stepped in. For example, in Wisconsin, service was abandoned on the spur line between Sparta and Viroqua, as well as between Madison and Mineral Point. However, a succession of short-line operators were created, usually with local government's assistance to ensure that shippers who relied on local rail service were

A former Milwaukee Road GP9, now operating under the Wisconsin and Calumet Railroad (WICT) in Clarno, Wisconsin. *Photo Credit: Richard Kundert.*

not left high and dry. The Chicago, Madison and Northern Railroad (CM&N) was created to serve the aforementioned lines in 1980, using three locomotives and borrowing rolling stock from other railroads. The CM&N Railroad lasted only a few years before other short lines like the Wisconsin and Calumet and its successor the Wisconsin and Southern assumed the responsibility of serving local industries, especially in the areas west of Madison toward Reedsburg, Wisconsin, and around Green Bay. As of this writing, there are two primary short-line operators left in the Badger State, Wisconsin and Southern, now operated by Watco, and the Wisconsin Central Railroad, operated as a subsidiary of Canadian National, as well as smaller lines like the Escabana & Lake Superior Railroad and Fox Valley & Lake Superior Railroads.

By the middle of the 1990s, not a single Granger Road stood in the Midwest. In some cases, their names and their former rail networks lived on, but all their motive power and rolling stock were left to rot or snapped up by the new mega-railroads. However, the influence of the Grangers stands tall over the United States even today. Their power and influence led to a revolution in legislative regulation of industry. The model of the Granger Laws throughout the Midwest gave the federal government a template with which to create the ICC, one of the first real regulatory bodies to hold sway over an entire industry. The railroads that the Grangers fought against became the lifeblood of the Midwest and were, by the 1980s, the canary in the coal mine for a system of regulations that had become too cumbersome to function in a modern economy. However, for Granger Roads, the damage was done, and they, like the organization that opposed them, faded into history.

8

THE GRANGER LEGACY

The Granger railroads may no longer be in business, their dominant market share in Wisconsin, Minnesota, Iowa and Illinois usurped by the likes of Canadian Pacific and Kansas City (CPKC), Burlington Northern Santa Fe (BSNF) and Union Pacific (UP), but their development and the legislative movements that hoped to rein them in have left an indelible mark on both the Midwest and the entire nation. There are echoes of the greatness of the Granger Roads to be seen throughout both the physical and political landscape of modern America. Yet among the bike trails, in train museums and even on the occasional passenger service, the Granger Roads still stand as a monument to a transformative time more often than not forgotten and passed over by history books and in popular memory.

The regulation of the Grangers led to a revolutionary shift in American bureaucracy. The model of the ICC became mirrored in numerous regulatory bodies that were created to shift the burden of creating complex rules and guidelines for industries from the legislature to newly created regulatory organizations. The New Deal saw many of these regulatory agencies born out of the ashes of the Great Depression. The Securities and Exchange Commission (SEC) was created to regulate Wall Street while the National Labor Relations Board (NLRB) was created to settle disputes between management and organized labor. Later in the twentieth century, the Environmental Protection Agency (EPA) was created to halt the pollution of the environment. Perhaps the most apt comparison would be the Civil

Aeronautics Board (CAB), created in 1938 as a mirror of the ICC to control and regulate the rapidly burgeoning air travel industry.

Much like the ICC, the CAB was born out of a desire to create order in an industry that was brand new, like the railroads in the mid-nineteenth century, and posed new challenges for the nation to ensure safety and promote economic equity. As the ICC did, the CAB had the regulatory power to determine which airlines flew to which destinations and what they could charge for rates. The CAB also determined safety standards for airlines and monitored the implementation of all of these rules in further allusions to its predecessor. Around the same time that the Staggers Act was finding its genesis, Congress decided airlines could also benefit from deregulation. In 1978, Congress passed the Airline Deregulation Act, which phased out the CAB's rate and route regulations; the monitoring of airline safety regulations had been moved to the Federal Aviation Administration during the 1950s.

Deregulation of the airline industry initially seemed to produce drastically different results. There was an airline boom in the 1970s and early 1980s. According to Bureau of Transportation data in 1970, 39 air carriers were operating within the United States flying 2,690 aircraft. However, in 1980, that number had skyrocketed to 66 carriers flying 2,818 aircraft. This massive influx of new air transportation companies was exactly what deregulation had hoped to achieve; however, the prosperity was short-lived, and the airline market corrected itself within a decade. As rates plummeted due to high competition between new airlines and established companies, many airlines that were in poor economic condition soon failed, and several of the upstarts lasted only a few years. Even some of the more long-standing airlines like Braniff fell in the race to the bottom. Only those airlines that could ride out the price wars survived through their own strong networks and sheer size and economies of scale.

As the initial phase of airline deregulation faded, it became clear that airline deregulation was heading toward a similar end as railroad deregulation, consolidation. Companies with storied histories like Eastern Airlines and Pan-Am were forced into mergers or bankruptcy. Today, four major airlines control 68 percent of the United States airline market share: United Airlines, Delta Airlines, American Airlines and Southwest Airlines. This concentration of market share is mirrored by the similar concentration of the modern railroad market between BNSF, CSX, Norfolk and Southern, CPKC, Canadian National and Union Pacific. According to the Association of American Railroads, the six Class I railroads in the

United States account for 94 percent of all rail revenue generated within the country.

In 1980, following the successful deregulation movements in the rail and air transport industries, the federal government passed the Motor Carrier Act. Essentially a copy-paste of the Staggers Act but aimed at trucking, the Motor Carrier Act allowed trucking companies to set their own rates and negotiate contracts and removed other restrictions on competition. The act proved to be more successful than its counterparts and resulted in a flourishing, more efficient industry. According to a 1983 Government Accountability Office Report, in 1977, there were sixteen thousand carriers registered with the ICC; however, by 1982, that number had risen to over twenty-five thousand due to decreased barriers to entry. The report further noted that rates had fallen anywhere from 10 percent to 40 percent but that there were no indications that these rate reductions were due to unfair business practices by larger firms as a means to price out competitors—rather they were the result of natural competition.

Of the three major modes of non-water transport—rail, trucking and airlines—highway transport has emerged from the decades of deregulation as the poster child of the movement. In 2020, in the midst of the COVID-19 pandemic when supply chains were front-page news, *Business Insider* characterized trucking, an industry with over 200,000 trucking firms (most of which were small-time companies operating less than six tractor-trailers), as a "perfect competition," an economic term for industries in which there is so much choice between relatively equal buyers and sellers that the price will naturally find its lowest equilibrium point. Indeed, according to the same articles, costs have drastically dropped for shippers and buyers alike, allowing the modern e-commerce and big-box store economic models to thrive in the twenty-first century. Similar movements are happening in the modern railroads, with "precision railroading" emphasizing larger trains and fewer train crews to drive efficiency in order to provide a cheaper service; however, the jury is still out on precision scheduled railroading.

Despite the far-reaching political and economic legacies of the Granger Roads, there are also physical reminders of their long tenure. As discussed in earlier chapters, many of the earliest railroad ventures in the Midwest and western states involved large land grants from the federal government to railroads to provide for rights-of-way and to help fund the construction of railroads through land sales. One major and unforeseen consequence of this land distribution was that the remaining federal land was left in a checkerboard state. In many cases, crossing the corners where two private parcels meet with two public parcels, a process described literally as "corner crossing," is illegal due to the way most state's trespass laws have been written up.

According to a report compiled by hunting mapping company OnX, there are currently 9.5 million acres of public land, mostly in the far western states, sitting landlocked by private parcels without any public road or trail access, with nearly half of the total landlocked acreage located in Wyoming and Montana alone. OnX also notes that landowners had historically granted permission more frequently to hunters; however, as ownership practices have changed, this process has become increasingly less common.

Some states are offering solutions to the corner crossing issue. According to the Mirr Ranch Group, a brokerage for finding ranch properties, South Dakota has a law on the books from the initial settlement of the state that created a sixty-six-foot-wide public access corridor along all section lines within the state. However, there are currently ongoing court cases testing whether or not that law would allow for public hunting access. In states like Wyoming, hunters have even attempted to create homemade ladder bridges over private property to get from one public parcel to another. One group of hunters who attempted this method of corner crossing

United States map of land grants to railroads, 1878. *David Rumsey Map Archive.*

were brought up on trespassing charges. The men were initially cleared of charges; however, they were later sued by the property owner for violating the airspace above his property. In 2023, a decision was made by the U.S. District Court in Wyoming in which the hunters were handed an unexpected win. The judge noted the historical ties to the railroad in his decision, stating:

> *To promote westward expansion in the 19th century the federal government encouraged the construction of rail lines through the West by granting every other 640-acre parcel along rail corridors to a railroad company. The hope was that the lands remaining with the government would increase in value as the companies built rail lines, which the government would later sell at high prices. The plan was successful further east, but the government struggled to sell the lands in the arid West. The result of this failed venture is the checkerboard pattern of public and private land that now plagues much of the West.*

The judge in the case found that, based on previous case law, individuals have a right to reasonably access public property, and that while private property owners do have a right to the airspace above their property, corner crossing on foot without actually contacting the private property was not trespassing. While the federal government likely could not have foreseen the consequences of the land grants on future property law, the very existence of the land ownership checkerboard in the West is a physical reminder of the federal government's driving ambition to fulfill manifest destiny through railroad expansion.

An even more evident physical reminder of the railroads, in particular the Granger Roads, are the unused rail beds they left behind. According to Assistant Professor of Economics at Vassar Dustin Frye, from their peak in 1916, U.S. railroads abandoned nearly 40 percent of the 250,000-mile network throughout the rest of the twentieth century. With approximately 100,000 miles of unused railbed, the question quickly became, What can be done with this unused land? One answer was legislated into existence in the 1980s and quickly became a popular answer in the Midwest: the Rails-to-Trails Act. During the 1970s, in the years leading up to the Staggers Act, railroads were abandoning thousands of miles of line per year, attempting to remain afloat by casting off routes that were unprofitable and maintenance-intensive. As a result, the federal government realized the need to step in to help facilitate the transfer of these corridors.

The first attempt by Congress to utilize newly abandoned rights-of-way was the Railroad Revitalization and Regulatory Reform Act, which forestalled the full abandonment of a line for 180 days to allow for finding a "public use" of the line. This was followed by an amendment to the National Trails System Act in 1983, which allowed for the conversion of a line that would otherwise be abandoned into a multiuse trail that could be preserved or reconverted to a rail line in the future if deemed necessary. The idea was nothing new; purchases of former lines had been negotiated in the past and turned into trails for some time before 1983, but the Rail Banking Act gave the government a new tool in order to streamline the process. Railroad rights-of-way conversions to recreational trails make excellent choices. Generally speaking, railroad grades are fairly flat, with any climbs being gradual and easily ridden or hiked. They also tend to connect small towns, providing an economic lifeline to towns that have otherwise been left behind by the departing railroads. While there are still ongoing and significant legal issues regarding who has the right to land after it has been abandoned by the railroad, turning former railroad lines into recreational trails has become a common way to use the former infrastructure.

Perhaps fittingly, as the Granger Roads were often trailblazers in their time, a former Granger line is often considered the first "Rail Trail" in the nation. Extending thirty-two miles on former CNW lines, the Sparta-Elroy Trail was established in 1966. The route was part of the famed Dakota 400 service and featured three tunnels atop some of the rolling hills of the region, the longest of which stretches nearly three-quarters of a mile. According to the Wisconsin DNR, hikers were the first to enjoy the trail, but by 1970, the length of the trail had been graded with limestone, providing easier access to cyclists. By the 1970s, forty thousand people were enjoying the beauty of the driftless region annually, a number that would only rise throughout the years.

Over time, the Rail-to-Trail movement in Wisconsin gathered steam. During the early 1990s, the 22-mile 400 State Trail was added, connecting Reedsburg to Elroy and the terminus of the famed Sparta-Elroy Trail, the name of the trail a clear homage to the heritage of the corridor on which it was built. The CNW had previously abandoned the lines between Elroy and Reedsburg; however, the Wisconsin and Southern Railroad still use the former lines going south from Reedsburg to Madison. The Hillsboro State Trail runs along the railbed of the 4.8-mile former Hillsboro and Northeastern Railway, connecting the small town of Hillsboro to the

A cyclist traverses one of the tunnels along the former CNW mainline between Sparta and Elroy, Wisconsin. *Wisconsin Bike Federation via Creative Commons, https://creativecommons.org/licenses/by-sa/2.0/.*

400 Trail at Union Center, Wisconsin. The railroad and its namesake community claimed at various times this was the shortest railroad in the nation; however, this fact is highly debated and unlikely to be true. Eventually, further connections were made along the existing active railbed from Sparta to La Crosse, Wisconsin, and as far north as Trempealeau, creating a continuous rail trail that runs approximately 100 miles between Reedsburg and Trempealeau.

As of the spring of 2024, the Wisconsin state trail network listed 39 trails as "Rail Trails," encompassing a total of 1,198 miles of recreational trail throughout the state. Wisconsin, however, is not alone in its wholesale endorsement of the Rail Trails; the other Granger states have enthusiastically endorsed the program as well. According to Rail to Trails Conservancy, Iowa has 101 trails that run for 1,009 miles, and Illinois' system of 89 trails runs for 1,082 miles, but it is the state of Minnesota that beats out all of the other Grangers with 92 trails stretching out for a staggering 2,240 miles.

While passenger rail has significantly declined under the management of Amtrak, many of the famous Granger routes still exist. Amtrak pays tribute to the Chicago, Burlington and Quincy's groundbreaking Zephyr with the California Zephyr Route, as well as carrying on the later Burlington Northern's Empire Builder route across the northern Rocky Mountains. Union Pacific, as well as many other modern Class I railroads, paint some of their locomotives in "heritage" liveries to pay homage to the railroads hoovered up in the years after deregulation. However, the Granger Roads' arms race for higher speeds and more luxurious travel, while short-lived, may have been prophetic, as recent plans, including those from the High-Speed Rail Alliance as well as the State of Wisconsin, call for a high-speed rail corridor to connect Chicago, Madison and Minneapolis, along much of the original Milwaukee Road line, as well as many of the now abandoned east–west corridors from roads like the CNW and CB&Q. Only a small handful of the once great Granger routes survive in twenty-first-century passenger rail service, yet the echoes are there for those who know where to find them.

The question must be asked, Where does the Grange fit into the twenty-first century? The National Grange, as an organization, has lost the outsized political weight that it wielded over 150 years ago. However, according to the *Journal of Proceedings* from the 2023 national convection, the Grange has at the very least stabilized its membership base after years of decline. The national president of the organization, Betsy Huber, noted that for the first time since 1955, nationally, the Grange posted two consecutive years of net membership gain. The organization is still based on the same beliefs that made it such a powerful force in the late nineteenth century. Their current mission statement reads, "The Grange strengthens individuals, families, and communities through grassroots action, service, education, advocacy, and agricultural awareness." However, the demographics of the United States in the 2020s are vastly different from the 1870s, and as such, the organization will likely never wield the same political strength it once did.

Yet the Grangers are inextricably linked to the way the twenty-first-century rail network has developed in the United States. According to the CIA World Factbook, the United States possesses by far the largest rail network of any nation in the world at over 290,000 kilometers, or around 180,000 miles. The next closest nation, Russia, has only 150,000 kilometers. Yet the United States has consistently ranked among the worst passenger rail networks in the world. According to Amtrak, in 2023 there were 28.6 million passenger trips across the network, whereas Germany's Deutsche Bahn served nearly 2 billion passengers in the same time on a network that is 260,000 kilometers smaller.

Union Pacific's heritage liveried 1995 locomotive painted in CNW colors. *Tyler Silvest via Creative Commons, https://creativecommons.org/licenses/by-sa/2.0/.*

So why would the United States, a pioneer in rail travel in possession of one of the most extensive rail networks, have such a weak passenger network? The answer lies in the ashes of the 1970s and the creation of Amtrak. When created, Amtrak was given a monopoly over the services it chose to absorb. The law itself states, "No railroad or any other person may, without the consent of the Corporation, conduct intercity rail transport service over any route over which the Corporation is performing scheduled intercity rail passenger service." This meant that once Amtrak chose a route, there would be no competition. As was the case with rail deregulation, airline deregulation and trucking deregulation, when competition was allowed, services generally became more profitable and more affordable and service quality rose. However, as can be seen through this work, when the ICC was stifling competition, rates remained high and service quality was relatively low, and with Amtrak having no competitors, the same result is occurring.

Another aspect that has hamstrung Amtrak in its ability to serve rail passengers is their reliance, outside of the northeastern corridor between Washington, D.C., and Boston, on infrastructure from other railroad companies. This also was codified by the Rail Passenger Service Act in

High Speed Rail Alliance map of proposed services throughout the Midwest. *High Speed Rail Alliance.*

1970, which states, "The Corporation may contract with railroads or with regional transportation agencies for the use of tracks and other facilities." As reported in the 2022 Company Profile, Amtrak operates a route network of 21,400 miles; however, only 623.1 miles are wholly owned and operated by Amtrak, with another 229 miles operated and maintained by Amtrak through lease agreements with other railroads. This leaves Amtrak at the mercy of the major freight railroads in terms of infrastructure maintenance, updates and expansion.

This is further complicated by the introduction of precision scheduled railroading (PSR) to many of the Class I railroads. According to the

Government Accountability Office, six of the seven largest freight railroads have reported implementing this strategy, which simply, according to the GAO, means, "(1) reductions in staff, (2) longer trains, and (3) reductions in assets such as locomotives. For example, the overall number of staff among the seven largest freight railroads (known as Class I) decreased by about 28 percent from 2011 through 2021. Further, all seven railroads said they have increased the length of trains in recent years." However, much of the infrastructure of American railroads has remained the same, such as sidings (tracks that allow a train to "pull over") and rail yards, as well as the profiling of curves and so on.

According to a 2023 "Host Railroad Report Card" from Amtrak, five of the six graded freight railroads caused at least 1,000 minutes of delay for 10,000 train miles traveled, with the worst offenders causing more than 1,350 minutes per 10,000 train miles. Amtrak asserts this is due to the illegal preferencing of freight movements over Amtrak, the reverse of what federal law requires. Amtrak further states in the report card that the Department of Justice has chosen to enforce the laws on Amtrak preference only once in over forty years, essentially giving the freight railroads a green light to continue disrupting passenger service without any fear of repercussion. Amtrak claims that the longer trains, a direct result of PSR, no longer fit in some sidings, making it even harder for Amtrak to get preference. In the 2023 report, Amtrak states that none of its long-distance routes could achieve an 80 percent target for on-time performance and that in total there were 900,000 delay minutes experienced by Amtrak trains throughout 2023.

The value of deregulation in saving the U.S. rail network cannot be understated; however, the regulatory system that created the need for Amtrak, the ICC and its predecessor Granger Laws produced a situation where government-supported passenger service became subservient to freight rails both in need for infrastructure creation and improvement as well as preferential access to that infrastructure. The freight railroads are acting in their best interest; they see little benefit in running the passenger services their predecessors cast off to the Amtrak corporation more than fifty years ago, and there is little value gained from their trackage rights. According to the 2017 Host Report Card, Amtrak paid approximately $142 million to freight railroads for track rights; in the same period, Union Pacific alone brought in $2.2 billion in revenue. Amtrak's payments likely do not constitute enough of an economic incentive for the railroads to prioritize their service either.

A new Brightline passenger trainset undergoing testing. *BBT609 (Flikr) via Creative Commons, https://creativecommons.org/licenses/by-sa/2.0/.*

There are precious few rail lines that are likely to begin on non–Amtrak served routes either, which would drive competition. In the twenty-first century, the major success in new private intercity service is Brightline. In 2018, Brightline began a line connecting two of the most popular vacation destinations in Florida, Orlando and Miami, with high-speed rail, completing the project in 2023. As of 2024, the company operates sixteen round trips between the two cities daily and has recently proposed a line connecting Los Angeles to Las Vegas. Aside from Brightline, there are no major companies that operate any intercity passenger service. The barrier to entry is extremely high. As discussed in previous chapters, railroads are one of the only transportation modes responsible for their entire infrastructure, both at the terminal destinations and between them.

The lack of competition on Amtrak routes means that the most profitable and popular routes are off-limits to private competition, and Amtrak has no real financial reason to improve their services—if they would even be able to given the reluctance of the freight railroads to provide them access or the proper infrastructure for high-speed rail in the first place. In a way, this is right where the Grangers would have wanted passenger rail to be going as far back as the Omaha Platform's call for state-run railroads; however, the Grangers likely could not have envisaged the final product being as sparse and poorly equipped.

The Grangers' advocacy in the 1870s could hardly have envisioned a world in which the freight railroads would be brought to near death by overregulation, and then return to a position of flaunting federal regulation with little impunity and only thought for the bottom line. Nevertheless, the framework that they, through their network of farmer advocates and elected officials, created in the Midwest in the 1870s provided an efficient, popular and effective framework to bring the railroad barons to heel at the height of their power. However, left unchecked, the regulatory agency that emerged from the populist fervor, the ICC, ended up becoming bloated and ineffectual, slowed down by red tape and a reluctance to quickly adapt to changing times. This led to an industry drowning in red tape, saved at the last moment by a Congress willing to deregulate transportation en masse.

In the Passenger Rail Act, Congress noted the value of the passenger rail network in the United States, saying, "The Congress finds that modern, efficient, intercity railroad passenger service is a necessary part of a balanced transportation system." However, in the more than half a century since the act's passage, Congress has been reluctant to give any teeth to the enforcement of this pledge. The result is a rail network nearly

A Chicago and Northwestern F unit leaving Madison, Wisconsin, in 1973, with the capital in the background. *Photo credit: Mark Llanuza.*

double that of the next largest industrial nation with a passenger rail network near the bottom of all industrial nations. If the Grangers could see the rail network that they helped shape, it is entirely likely they would feel the entire process had failed, that the ideals of the post–Civil War era of rail regulation were meant to create a fair framework that did not harm the railroad, passenger or shipper. Instead, they helped create a system of railroads too big to fail, focused only on bottom lines, all too reminiscent of the railroads they were fighting. However, gone are the midwestern roads, replaced now with networks that span the entire continent, moving quantities of freight unimaginable in the nineteenth century. Not all can be blamed on the Grangers—new modes of transport relegated railroads to moving bulk goods rather than being a universal solution. Yet one must wonder what riding a train in 2024 would have looked like had it not been for a few farmers banding together in the 1800s to fight the goliath of the railroads with the most American of ideals, that no man, no company, is above the law, and that in America it is not the rich or powerful who retain the right to rule but the people.

BIBLIOGRAPHY

1. *Land Grants, Speculation and the Rise of the Early Railroads*

Baldwin, W.W. *Chicago, Burlington & Quincy Railroad Company—Documentary History*. Chicago, Burlington and Quincy Railroad Company, 1928.

Belvidere Standard. "Railroad Celebration at Joliet." October 21, 1851.

Boscobel Broad Axe. "Great Railroad Suit." February 1, 1865.

Brooke, Kathleen. "Erie Canal, United States." Building the World, May 8, 2012. https://blogs.umb.edu.

Buffalo Commercial. "Chicago and Rock Island Railroad." October 19, 1852.

———. "Western Railroads." October 16, 1848.

Canal Corridor Association. "Canal History—I & M Canal." Illinois & Michigan Canal National Heritage Area, 2023. https://iandmcanal.org.

Davenport Weekly Gazette. "Hurra for the Missouri!" September 22, 1853.

———. "Local Matters." June 23, 1853.

———. "The Mississippi and Missouri Railroad Company." February 3, 1853.

Ellis, David Maldwyn. "Railroad Land Grant Rates, 1850–1945." *Journal of Land & Public Utility Economics* 21, no. 3 (1945): 207–22.

Encyclopædia Britannica. "Baltimore and Ohio Railroad | History & Facts." https://www.britannica.com.

Environment & Society Portal. "US Government Land Grants: 'A Pleasure to Break the Wild Prairie.'" Rachel Carson Center for Environment and Society, March 19, 2020. https://www.environmentandsociety.org.

Federal Reserve Bank of St. Louis (FRED). "Miles of Railroad Built for United States." National Bureau of Economic Research. https://fred.stlouisfed.org.

Illinois Eighteenth General Assembly. An Act to Amend an Act Entitled "An Act to Amend the Charter of the Chicago and Aurora Railroad Company." 1853.

———. An Act to Amend the Charter of the Chicago and Aurora Railroad Company. 1854.

Illinois Ninth General Assembly. An Act to Incorporate the Galena and Chicago Union Rail Road Company. 1836.

Illinois Seventeenth General Assembly. An Act to Amend the Charter of the Aurora Branch Railroad Company. 1852.

Illinois Sixteenth General Assembly. An Act Granting a Charter to the Aurora Branch Railroad Company. 1849.

Illinois State Department. "Early Chicago, 1833–1871." www.ilsos.gov.

Illinois State Register. "Business on the Railroad." December 19, 1850.

———. "Chicago and Rock Island Railroad." March 20, 1851.

———. "Northern Railroad Matters." September 5, 1850.

———. "Workmen on the Aurora." August 30, 1850.

Independent. "Milwaukee and Watertown Railroad." January 3, 1856.

Janesville Daily Gazette. "Change of Name." June 9, 1859.

———. "Milwaukee and Prairie Du Chien Railway." July 12, 1861.

———. "Trustees Sale of the Chicago, St. Paul and Fond Du Lac Railroad." May 31, 1859.

Karamanski, Theodore. "Shipbuilding." www.encyclopedia.chicagohistory.org.

Kleist, Frederica. "Portage Canal." Portage Canal Society. http://portagecanal.org.

Library of Congress. "Today in History—August 24." https://www.loc.gov.

McBride, Sarah. "Fort Winnebago." Wisconsin Historical Society, August 8, 2017. https://www.wisconsinhistory.org.

Milwaukee Daily Sentinel. "Correspondence of the Sentinel and Gazette." February 16, 1847.

Milwaukee Historical Society. "Milwaukee Timeline | Milwaukee County Historical Society." https://milwaukeehistory.net.

New York State Canal Corporation. "Canal History—New York State Canals." www.canals.ny.gov.

North Iowa Times. "Anythings." June 12, 1861.

Racine Journal. "The Farm Mortgages." January 12, 1859.

Rock Island Weekly Argus. "Galena and Minnesota Packet Co." June 14, 1854.

Sauk County Standard. "Milwaukee and Watertown RR." November 5, 1854.

Semi-Weekly Wisconsin. "A Railroad Bugbear Put to Rest." April 17, 1867.

———. "The Railway System of Milwaukee." April 17, 1867.

St. Paul Weekly Minnesotan. "Facts and Fancies." March 18, 1854.

Stanford. "History of American Railroads." https://cs.stanford.edu.

Stratton, H.J. "The Northern Cross Railroad." *Journal of the Illinois State Historical Society* 28, no. 2 (1935): 5–52.

Syracuse Daily Courier and Union. "A Railroad Row at Milwaukee." March 10, 1858.

Taylor, George Rogers, and Henry David. *The Transportation Revolution: 1815–1860*. Holt, Rinehart and Winston, 1951.

Telegraph Courier. "First Rail Road Ride in Wisconsin." November 29, 1850.

United States Census Bureau. "Abstract of the Returns of the Fifth Census." Washington: Duff Green, 1832.

———. "Return of the Whole Number of Persons within the Several Districts of the United States," December 8, 1801.

United States Census Bureau, Census History Staff. "May 2018—History—U.S. Census Bureau." www.census.gov.

United States National Archives. "Homestead Act (1862)." National Archives, July 29, 2021. https://www.archives.gov.

Watertown Chronicle. "What the Interior Needs." January 5, 1853.

Waukesha Plaindealer. "Rail-Road Consolidation." September 30, 1856.

Weekly Wisconsin. "Milwaukee and Watertown Railroad." May 11, 1853.

———. "Railroad Meeting." December 1, 1847.

———. "St. Ann's Female Seminary Association." September 5, 1855.

Western Carolinian. "Internal Improvements." October 16, 1827.

Wilm, Julius, Robert K. Nelson and Justin Madron, "Homesteading." In *American Panorama*, ed. Robert K. Nelson and Edward L. Ayers. https://dsl.richmond.edu/panorama/homesteading/.

Wisconsin Department of Natural Resources. "Overview of Metallic Mining in Wisconsin | | Wisconsin DNR." dnr.wisconsin.gov.

Wisconsin State Journal. "Milwaukee and Mississippi Railroad." January 17, 1861.

———. "Milwaukee, Watertown, and Madison Railroad." March 3, 1857.

———. "Notice of the Change of the Name of the Milwaukee and St Paul Railway Company." February 21, 1874.

———. "Opening of the Milwaukee and Mississippi Railroad." April 17, 1857.

Wisconsin State Register. "Circular: Office of Galena and Chicago Union R.R." November 15, 1862.

2. The Civil War and Postwar Period: Agriculture and Rail Monopolies

Amerman, John W. "Sixth Annual Report of the Chicago and North Western Railway Company." May 31, 1865. Google Books. https://books.google.com.

"Annual Report of the Chicago and North Western Railway Company for the Fourteenth Fiscal Year." May 31, 1873. HathiTrust. https://www.hathitrust.org.

Arrington, Benjamin T. "Industry and Economy during the Civil War (U.S. National Park Service)." National Park Service, www.nps.gov.

Buffalo Commercial. "New York Market." February 3, 1863.

Centralia Sentinel. "Kohl & Warner Dealers in Dry Goods." September 3, 1863.

Constitution Society. "1862, May 20 - 12 Stat. 392, Homestead Act." U.S. Government Legislation and Statutes. https://digitalcommons.csumb.edu/hornbeck_usa_2_d/12/.

Deere Brand Microsite. "John Deere." https://about.deere.com.

Drury, George. "Milwaukee Road History." Trains.com, November 13, 2021. https://www.trains.com.

Fite, Emerson D. "The Agricultural Development of the West during the Civil War." *Quarterly Journal of Economics* 20, no. 2 (February 1906): 259.

Gallman, Robert E., and John Joseph Wallis. *American Economic Growth and Standards of Living before the Civil War*. Chicago: University of Chicago Press, 1992.

Ginzberg, Eli. "The Economics of British Neutrality during the American Civil War." *Agricultural History* 10, no. 4 (1936): 147–56.

Library of Congress. "The Transcontinental Railroad | History of Railroads and Maps | Articles and Essays | Railroad Maps, 1828-1900 | Digital Collections | Library of Congress." https://www.loc.gov.

McCabe, James D. *History of the Grange Movement*. National Publishing Company, 1873.

McCormick. "History." https://www.mccormick.it/us/history/.

McNamara, Robert. "Invention of the McCormick Reaper." ThoughtCo. https://www.thoughtco.com/.

Milwaukee and St. Paul Railway Company. *Fifth Annual Report of the Milwaukee and St. Paul Railway Company*. Wisconsin Book and Job Printing House, 1868.

Mitchell, Samuel Augustus. "Railroad Map U.S." David Rumsey Map Collection. https://www.davidrumsey.com.

Morning Democrat. "Commercial." December 29, 1871.

———. "Markets by Telegraph." December 21, 1870.

National Park Service. "Facts—the Civil War (U.S. National Park Service)." https://www.nps.gov

North Iowa Times. "Commercial." September 5, 1860.

———. "Commercial and Financial Report." July 25, 1860.

———. "Home and Other Items." September 25, 1861.

———. "Weather, Markets &C." February 25, 1863.

Pope, Nancy. "The Story of the Pony Express." Smithsonian National Postal Musuem. https://postalmuseum.si.edu.

"Report of the Board of Directors of the Chicago, Burlington, and Quincy Railroad Company." February 24, 1875. Google Books. https://books.google.com.

Risch, Erna. *Quartermaster Support of the Army*. U.S. Army Center of Military History, 1989.

Sioux City Journal. "The Daily Journal." March 14, 1872.

Stewart, James. "The Economics of American Farm Unrest, 1865–1900." Economic History Association. https://eh.net.

Thirty-Second Congress of the United States. An Act Making Appropriations for the Support of the Army for the Year Ending Fourteenth of June, One Thousand Eight Hundred and Fifty-Four. 1853.

U.S. Army Heritage and Education Center. "Food and Foraging." https://ahec.armywarcollege.edu.

Union Pacific Railway. "Timeline | History of Union Pacific." https://www.up.com/timeline/index.cfm.

United States Department of Agriculture. "Crop Production Historical Track Records." April 2019. https://www.nass.usda.gov

United States National Archives. "Pacific Railway Act (1862)." August 10, 2021. https://www.archives.gov

United States Post Office. "Overland Mail to California in the 1850s - Postal History - Who We Are - About.usps.com." https://about.usps.com.

United States Post Office Historian. *Mail by Rail*. United States Post Office, 2008.

Washington Union. "Senator Douglas's Speech." October 29, 1846.

White, John H. *The American Railroad Passenger Car*. Johns Hopkins University Press, 1985.

Whitney, Asa. *A Project for a Railroad to the Pacific*. George W. Wood, 1849.

William, Wright Baldwin. *Chicago, Burlington & Quincy Railroad Company Documentary History*. R.R. Donnelley & Sons Company, 1928.

3. The First Granger Laws and the Panic of 1873

Chicago Weekly Post. "Chicago Weekly Post," November 6, 1873.

Clinton Register. "News Summary," October 24, 1873.

Daily Pantagraph. "THE RAILROADS and the COMMISSIONERS." July 31, 1871.

Dodgeville Chronicle. "The Latest News," May 8, 1874.

Glasner, David, and Thomas F. Cooley. *Business Cycles and Depressions: An Encyclopedia*. Garland Publishing 1997.

Hearn, A.S. "Current Items." *Dodgeville Chronicle*, May 22, 1874.

Illinois General Assembly.. *An Act Regulating the Receiving, Transportation, and Delivery of Grain by Railroad Corporations, and Defining the Duties of Such Corporations with Respect Thereto.* 1871.

Iowa County Democrat. "Governor Taylor—A Pen Portrait of the Next Governor of Wisconsin." December 11, 1873.

Kingston Daily Freeman. "TELEGRAPH: Regular Dispatches to the Daily Freeman." September 22, 1873.

Lawrence Daily Journal. "BY TELEGRAPH." January 28, 1874.

McCabe, James D. *History of the Grange Movement*. National Publishing Company, 1874.

Mineral Point Weekly Tribune. "Some Railroad Statistics," February 23, 1876.

Minnesota Legislature. *AN ACT for the REGULATION OF RAILROAD COMPANIES*. 1885.

———. *An Act to Provide for the Appointment of a Railroad Commissioner, and Prescribing His Duties.* 1871.

Morning Democrat. "Iowa," June 22, 1871.

Nashville Journal. "Local Jottings," August 5, 1871.

New-York Tribune. "The Railroad Law." September 5, 1874.

Rock Island Argus. "Legislative Correspondence." March 23, 1871.

Southern Argus. "NEW SECRET SOCIETY—the PATRONS of HUSBANDRY." April 7, 1870.

Star Tribune. "Railroad Tariffs." February 17, 1871.

Watertown News. "The New Railroad Law." March 5, 1876.

Western Rural. "The Grange." August 19, 1876.

———. "Railroad Monopoly." August 19, 1876.

Wisconsin State Journal. "The Legislature of 1875." January 12, 1875.

———. "RAILROADS VS. PEOPLE." April 8, 1874.

———. "The Vance Bill." February 16, 1876.

Wisconsin State Legislature. *An Act Relating to Railroads, Express, and Telegraph Companies in the State of Wisconsin*. https://docs.legis.wisconsin.gov.

Wisconsin Supreme Court. "Attorney General v. Chicago & Northwestern Railroad Company." Wisconsin Court System. https://www.wicourts.gov.
Wood County Reporter. "THE NEWS." January 29, 1874.

4. National Railroad Reform Arrives

Annual Report of the Board of Directors of the Chicago, Burlington, and Quincy Railway. Culver, Page, Hoyne, and Co. Printers, 1877.
Annual Report of the Chicago and North Western Railway Company for the Fortieth Fiscal Year. J.C. Winship Company, 1899.
Annual Report of the Chicago and Northwestern Railway. John W. Ammerman, 1875.
Annual Report of the Chicago and Northwestern Railway Company. John W. Ammerman, 1865.
Bloomfield Vindicator. "Miscellaneous." July 30, 1887.
Blue Mound Sun. "News of the Week." June 23, 1887.
Carthage Press. "The Granger Railroad Law." February 10, 1876.
Champaign Daily Gazette. "Seems a Drastic Measure." June 12, 1890.
Chicago, Burlington & Quincy Railroad Company v. Iowa, 94 U.S. 155 (1876).
Collins, Wayne. "Trusts and the Origins of Antitrust Legislation." *Fordham Law Review* 81, no. 5 (2019): 2279–348.
Dempsey, Paul Stephen. "The Rise and Fall of the Interstate Commerce Commission: The Tortuous Path from Regulation to Deregulation of America's Infrastructure." *Marquette Law Review* 95, no. 4 (January 2012): 1151.
Fifth Annual Report of the Milwaukee and St. Paul Railway Company. Evening Wisconsin Book and Job Printing House, 1868.
Forty-Eighth Annual Report of the Board of Directors of the Chicago, Burlington, and Quincy Railroad Company. Henry O. Shepard Company, 1902.
Fourteenth Annual Report of the Chicago, Milwaukee, and St. Paul Railway Company. Cramer, Aikens & Cramer Printers, 1877.
Goldin, Claudia, and Gary D. Libecap. *The Regulated Economy a Historical Approach to Political Economy*. University of Chicago Press, 1994.
Historical Statistics of the United States 1789–1945. U.S. Government Printing Office, 1949.
ICC v. Alabama Midland Railway Co., 168 U.S. 144 (1897).
ICC v. Cincinnati, N.O. & Texas Pacific Ry. Co., 167 U.S. 479 (1897).
Inter Ocean. "Trade Between States." December 22, 1886.

Jasper Weekly Courier. "Topics of the Day." April 15, 1887.
Lawrence Standard. "Legislative Control of Corporations." August 31, 1877.
Missoulian. "Morgan-Hill Meeting." October 17, 1901.
Morning Democrat. "Office of the M&M Railroad Company." June 6, 1857.
Munn v. Illinois, 94 U. S. 113 (1877).
National Archives. "Sherman Anti-Trust Act (1890)." https://www.archives.gov.
Peik v. Chicago & Northwestern Railway Company, 94 U.S. 164 (1876).
Perry County Monitor and Sun. "Miscellaneous." April 22, 1887.
Racine Journal. "Nebraska Letter." June 2, 1880.
Report of the Directors of the Chicago, Burlington & Quincy Railroad Company. Rounds & Kane, Book and Job Publishers, 1870.
Salt Lake Herald. "Good Bye to Bad Times." July 7, 1895.
San Francisco Examiner. "Our Trade in Danger." March 23, 1887.
St. Paul Globe. "Earnings on the Increase." November 10, 1899.
Star Tribune. "Stocks on Decline." May 21, 1907.
Statistical Abstract of the United States: 1925. United States Census Bureau, 1926.
Thirteenth Annual Report of the Directors of the Chicago, Milwaukee and St. Paul Railway Company. Cramer, Aikens and Cramer Printers, 1876.
Thirtieth Annual Report of the Board of Directors of the Chicago, Burlington, and Quincy Railroad Company. Shepard & Johnston Printers, 1883.
Thirty-Fifth Annual Report of the Board of Directors of the Chicago, Milwaukee and St. Paul Railway Company. Corbitt & Butterfield Printers, 1899.
Topeka Daily Capital. "Active Work." April 3, 1887.
Twentieth Annual Report of the Directors to the Stockholders of the Chicago, Rock Island, and Pacific Railway Company. Ryan & Hart Co., 1900.
United States v. E C. Knight Co., 156 U.S. 1 (1895)
Wabash, St. Louis & Pacific Railway Company v. Illinois, 118 U.S. 557 (1886)
Weekly Wisconsin. "Sold to the St Paul." September 27, 1890.
West-Jersey Pioneer. "The Granger Cases." March 8, 1877.
Wilson County Citizen. "Late News Items." July 29, 1887.

5. The Progressive Era and Advent of the Automobile

Bellis, Mary. "How Did the First American Highway Come About?" ThoughtCo. August 27, 2020. https://www.thoughtco.com.
Berkshire Eagle. "The Motor Wagon Race." August 28, 1897.
Brooklyn Daily Eagle. "President Has Won 4 Great Victories." July 1, 1906.

Capper's Weekly. "La Follette Called a Political Fakir by Senator Chester I. Long." October 18, 1906.

Chippewa Herald Telegram. "On the Merger Decision." March 16, 1904.

Daily Nonpareil. 1906. "Must Finish Its Work." July 27, 1906.

Dempsey, Paul. 2012. "The Rise and Fall of the Interstate Commerce Commission: The Tortuous Path from Regulation to Deregulation of America's Infrastructure Repository Citation." *Marquette Law Review* 95, no. 4 (Summer 2012) https://scholarship.law.marquette.edu.

Dispatch. "Secretary Knox Will Be Secretary." June 10, 1904.

Eagle River Review. "To Test Hill's Railroad Merger." March 17, 1902.

Encyclopædia Britannica. "United States—the Progressive Era." https://www.britannica.com.

Federal Reserve Bank of St. Louis. "Miles of Railroad Built for United States." National Bureau of Economic Research. https://fred.stlouisfed.org.

Fifty-Second Annual Report of the Chicago, Milwaukee, and St. Paul Railway Company. 1916.

Forty-Sixth Annual Report of the Chicago, Milwaukee, and St. Paul Railway Company. 1910.

Garner, James Wilford. "The Northern Securities Case." *The Annals of the American Academy of Political and Social Science* 24 (1904): 125–47.

Hawaiian Gazette. "The Horseless Carriages." July 17, 1896.

Hurdle, Fernando. "Research Guides: William McKinley Assassination: Topics in Chronicling America: Introduction." Library of Congress. https://guides.loc.gov/.

Iowa Railroad Commissioners. *Thirty-Ninth Annual Report of the Board of Railroad Commissioners*. State of Iowa, 1916.

———. *Thirty-Third Annual Report of the Board of Railroad Commissioners*. Emory English State Printer, 1910.

La Crosse Tribune. "ROADS PASS to NATION at NOON TODAY." December 28, 1917.

Lake Geneva Herald. "Write to Your Congressman." August 4, 1916.

Martin, Fernando. "Prices, Inflation since the Founding of the U.S." St. Louis Fed. www.stlouisfed.org.

Missouri State University. "Omaha Platform—1892." https://courses.missouristate.edu.

Morning Journal. "One Hundred Railroad Lawyers Meeting Daily to Find Flaw in Mann-Elkins Law." October 29, 1910.

National Constitution Center. "On This Day, Woodrow Wilson Seizes the Nation's Railroads | Constitution Center." https://constitutioncenter.org.

National Park Service. "1903—the First Flight—Wright Brothers National Memorial (U.S. National Park Service)." https://www.nps.gov.

Peoria Riverfront Museum. "Exhibits | Collections—DURYEA: America's First Car Company—Peoria Riverfront Museum." www.peoriariverfrontmuseum.org.

Ranch. "Horticulture," July 1, 1906.

Rock Island Argus. "M'ADOO TOOK ROADS LEVER HIGH TWELVE." December 28, 1917.

Saelee, Mike. "Research Guides: Eight Hour Day (1916): Topics in Chronicling America: Introduction." https://guides.loc.gov.

San Francisco Examiner. "Court May Forbid." March 15, 1904.

Sixty-Fifth Congress. *An Act to Provide for the Operation of Transportation Systems While under Federal Control, for Just Compensation of Their Owners, and for Other Purposes.* 1918.

Sixty-First Congress. *An Act to Create a Commerce Court, and to Amend the Act Entitled "an Act to Regulate Commerce."* 1910.

Smithsonian National Postal Museum. "The 1918 Flights | National Postal Museum." https://postalmuseum.si.edu.

Swinth, Kirsten. "The Square Deal: Theodore Roosevelt and the Themes of Progressive Reform." Gilder Lehman Institute of American History. https://www.gilderlehrman.org.

U.S. Capitol Visitor Center. "Representative William P. Hepburn of Iowa, Photograph, N.d." https://www.visitthecapitol.gov.

United States Census Bureau. "Statistics of Population—1900." 1901.

United States National Archives. "Hepburn Rate Bill." August 15, 2016. https://www.archives.gov.

Volti, Rudi. "A Century of Automobility." *Technology and Culture* 37, no. 4 (1996): 663.

Washington Times. "The Railroad Rate Bill," July 1, 1906.

Wisconsin Highway Commission. "Road Map of Wisconsin." 1916. https://wisconsindot.gov.

6. The Great Depression and the End of Railroad Monopoly

American Experience. "The Burlington Zephyr | American Experience | PBS." https://www.pbs.org.

Association of American Railroads. "Chronology of America's Freight Railroads." https://www.aar.org/.

Big Spring Daily Herald. "Rock Island Lines File Bankruptcy Proceedings." June 8, 1933.

Brooklyn Daily Eagle. "Chicago Creditor Sends St. Paul Ry. into Receivership." March 18, 1925.

Brooklyn Daily Times. "Air Line to Link Chile and Canada at First of Year." December 21, 1930.

———. "Safety of Travel in Air Forging to Perfection Mark." December 21, 1930.

Buffalo News. "The Background of Events." March 21, 1925.

Daily Nonpareil. "Blame School Bus Driver." October 25, 1937.

Dayskin Herald. "Rock Island 'Rocket' Flashes Through Plymouth." July 16, 1937.

Derleth, August. *The Milwaukee Road.* University of Iowa Press, 2002.

Eighty-Eighth Annual Report of the Board of Directors of the Chicago, Burlington and Quincy Railroad Company. 1941.

Eighty-Sixth Annual Report of the Board of Directors of the Chicago, Burlington, and Quincy Railroad Company. 1939.

Federal Highway Administration. "Public Road Mileage—VMT." Office of Highway Policy Information. November 7, 2014. https://www.fhwa.dot.gov.

Federal Reserve Bank of St. Louis. "Index of Farm Prices of Crops for United States." National Bureau of Economic Research. https://fred.stlouisfed.org.

Federico, Giovanni, and Paul Sharp. "The Cost of Railroad Regulation: The Disintegration of American Agricultural Markets in the Interwar Period." *The Economic History Review* 66, no. 4 (April 2013): 1017–38.

Fourteenth Annual Report of the Chicago, Milwaukee, St. Paul and Pacific Railway Company. 1947.

Franklin D. Roosevelt Presidential Library and Museum. "Great Depression Facts—FDR Presidential Library & Museum." https://www.fdrlibrary.org.

Gorman, Linda. "Fear of Failure, Bank Panics, and the Great Depression." National Bureau of Economic Research. May 1, 2020. https://www.nber.org.

Grant, H. Roger. *The North Western : A History of the Chicago & North Western Railway System.* Northern Illinois University Press, 1996.

Historical Statistics of the United States, Colonial Times to 1970. United States Census Bureau, 1975.

Historical Statistics of the United States, 1789–1945. United States Census Bureau, 1949.

Kenney Gazette. "Railway Makes Record." April 9, 1909.

La Crosse Tribune. "Approve Railroad Reorganization Plan." November 27, 1945.
———. "Milwaukee after Oriental Trade." January 18, 1909.
M'Alester News-Capital. "Rock Island Decreed Out of Receivership January 1." January 5, 1948.
Metra. "Chicago & North Western." https://metra.com.
Middleton, William D. *When the Steam Railroads Electrified*. Indiana University Press, 2001
Milwaukee Public Library. "Milwaukee Road Archives · MPL." www.mpl.org.
Mintz, Steven. "Statistics: The American Economy During the 1920s." Gilder Lehrman Institute of American History." www.gilderlehrman.org.
Moore, Lyndon, and Gertjan Verdickt. 2022. "Railroad Bailouts in the Great Depression." *ArXiv (Cornell University)*, May 25, 2022. https://arxiv.org/abs/2205.13025.
National Air and Space Museum. "The Evolution of the Commercial Flying Experience." https://airandspace.si.edu.
Olmstead, Alan L., and Paul W. Rhode. "The Diffusion of the Tractor in American Agriculture: 1910–60." *National Bureau of Economic Research*, January 2000.
Overton, Richard Cleghorn. *Burlington Route*. Knopf, 1965.
Standard Union. "Reorganization of Chicago, Milwaukee, and St. Paul Railway Company." November 21, 1925.
St. Louis Globe-Democrat. "Students on Tour Perish at Crossing." October 23, 1937.
Twelfth Annual Report of the Chicago, Milwaukee, St. Paul and Pacific Railway Company. 1939.
USDA. "Crop Production Historical Track Record." 2019. https://www.nass.usda.gov.
Wilkes-Barre Times Leader. "Railroads Are Cause of Stir." March 25, 1925.
Young, James. "Ripley Plan of Rail Mergers Attacked by Association of Security Owners and Executives." *St. Louis Globe-Democrat*, November 27, 1921.

7. Decline, Deregulation and Consolidation

Amarillo Globe-Times. "Introducing the Burlington Northern." March 3, 1970.
American Short Line Railroad Association. "1995 Annual Data Profile of the American Short Line and Regional Railroad Industry." Federal Railroad Administration. https://railroads.dot.gov.

Belleville Telescope. "Railroad People Are Still Arguing over Who Was to Blame for Rock Island Railroad Failure." April 24, 1980.

Belvidere Daily Republican. "Railway Merger Halt Approved." April 2, 1970.

Bowers, Peter M. *Boeing Aircraft since 1916*. U.S. Naval Institute Press, 1989.

Chicago, Milwaukee, St. Paul, and Pacific Annual Report 1968. 1968.

Chillicothe Constitution-Tribune. "Milwaukee Road Files Under Bankruptcy Act." December 26, 1977.

CNN Monday. "Canadian National Buys Wisconsin Central—Jan. 30, 2001." https://money.cnn.com.

Congressional Research Service. "Passenger Train Access to Freight Railroad Track." May 2, 2012. https://www.everycrsreport.com/.

Daily American Republic. "Rock Island, Labor Negotiators near Sale Problem Resolution." February 27, 1980.

Daily Mail. "Rock Island Merger Plan off Track." March 19, 1975.

Daily Telegram. "North Western Seeks to Discontinue '400' Trains." October 30, 1961.

Editors of the Consumer Guide. *American Cars of the 1950s*. Publications International, 2007.

Eighty-Fifth Congress of the United States. *An Act to Amend the Interstate Commerce Act, as Amended, so as to Strengthen and Improve the National Transportation System, and for Other Purposes*. 1958.

Goldman Sachs. "Goldman Sachs | Commemorates 150 Year History—Penn Central Bankruptcy Sends Shock Waves Through Commercial Paper Market." https://www.goldmansachs.com.

Historical Statistics of the United States, 1789–1945. United States Census Bureau, 1949.

Kokomo Tribune. "Union Pacific to Acquire Railroad." March 13, 1995.

La Crosse Tribune. "Railroad Officials Say Run Should Be Stopped." February 14, 1961.

Logansport Pharos-Tribune. "Rock Island Lines' Final Days Bitter." April 2, 1980.

Lydon, Christopher. "Amtrak Turns Back Court Challenges." *San Bernardino County Sun*, May 1, 1971.

1968 Annual Report of the Chicago, Burlington, and Quincy Railroad Company. 1968.

Palley, Joel. "Impact of the Staggers Rail Act of 1980." Federal Railway Administration, 2011. https://railroads.dot.gov.

Prater, Marvin, Adam Sparger, and Daniel O'Neil Jr. 2014. "Railroad Concentration, Market Shares, and Rates." Washington D.C.: United States Department of Agriculture.

Rail Passenger Service Act of 1970. 1970. Vol. 91–581.

Railroad Regulation Economic and Financial Impacts of the Staggers Rail Act of 1980. Government Accountability Office, 1990.

San Bernardino County Sun. "ICC Approves Santa Fe Merger." July 21, 1995.

Sunday Journal and Star. "Rocky Mountain Rocket 'Fizzles.'" October 16, 1966.

United States Bureau of the Census. Statistical Research Division. *The Statistical History of the United States, from Colonial Times to the Present—Historical Statistics of the United States, Colonial Times to 1970*. New York: Basic Books, 1976.

Weingroff, Richard. "Federal-Aid Highway Act of 1956: Creating the Interstate System." Federal Highway Administration. https://highways.dot.gov.

Wisconsin Department of Transportation. "Wisconsin Department of Transportation Freight Railroads." https://wisconsindot.gov.

8. The Granger Legacy

Amtrak. "Host Railroad Performance Report Card." December 31, 2023. https://www.amtrak.com.

Anderson, Kyle. "Amtrak Fiscal Year 2023: Ridership Exceeds Expectations as Demand for Passenger Rail Soars." Amtrak Media, November 30, 2023. https://media.amtrak.com.

Associated Press. "Rail Spikes Hammered, Bullet Train Being Built from Sin City to the City of Angels." *Orlando Sentinel*, April 22, 2024. https://www.orlandosentinel.com.

Association of American Railroads. "Data Center." https://www.aar.org.

Central Intelligence Agency. "Railways." https://www.cia.gov.

Federal Aviation Administration. "A Brief History of the FAA | Federal Aviation Administration." https://www.faa.gov.

Ferster, Andrea. "Rails-To-Trails Conversions: A Legal Review." Rails to Trails Conservancy, May 5, 2017. https://www.railstotrails.org.

Frye, Dustin. "Going Off the Rails: The Effect of Railroad Abandonments on Population and Industrial Decline." Vassar College, February 19, 2018. https://www.vassar.edu.

High Speed Rail Alliance. "High Speed Rail in Wisconsin." 2024. https://www.hsrail.org.

Howard, James. Motor Carrier Act of 1980, 94 Stat. 793 § (1980).

Krueger, Oliver. *THE INFLUENCE of the MOTOR CARRIER ACT of 1980 on TEAMSTERS' EMPLOYMENT*. Government Accountability Office, 1983.

Mirr, Ken. "Locked Out of the Land: Checkerboarding and Public Access in the American West." Mirr Ranch Group, February 28, 2023. www.mirrranchgroup.com.

National Air and Space Museum. "Airline Deregulation: When Everything Changed." https://airandspace.si.edu.

OnX Maps, and Theodore Roosevelt Conservation Partnership. "Off Limits but Within Reach, Unlocking the West's Inaccessible Public Lands." OnX Maps, 2017. https://www.onxmaps.com.

Premack, Rachel. "How a Little-Known 1980 Law Slashed Pay for Millions of Truck Drivers and Created Big-Box Retail as We Know It." Business Insider, July 25, 2020. https://www.businessinsider.com.

Rails to Trails Conservancy. "Top Trails in the United States." https://www.railstotrails.org.

Skavdahl, Scott. Iron Bar Holdings, LLC v. Cape (United States District Court, District of Wyoming May 26, 2023).

Union Pacific. "Union Pacific Reports Fourth Quarter and Full Year 2017 Results." January 25, 2018. https://www.up.com.

United States Bureau of the Census. Statistical Research Division. *The Statistical History of the United States, from Colonial Times to the Present = Historical Statistics of the United States, Colonial Times to 1970*. New York: Basic Books, 1976.

United States Department of Transportation. "Air Carrier Profile | Bureau of Transportation Statistics." Bureau of Transportation Statistics. 2024. https://www.bts.gov.

———. "OST_R | BTS | Transtats." Bureau of Transportation Statistics, January 31, 2024. https://www.transtats.bts.gov/.

Wisconsin Department of Natural Resources. "Sparta-Elory Story Map Journal." https://wi-dnr.maps.arcgis.com.

———. "StateTrailSystemFacts.pdf." https://widnr.widen.net.

Yahoo News. "German Railway Deutsche Bahn Reports €2.4bn Loss for 2023." March 21, 2024. https://www.yahoo.com.

ABOUT THE AUTHOR

Daniel Faas graduated from Luther College in Decorah, Iowa, in 2013 with a bachelor's degree in political science and classics with a minor in secondary education and an emphasis in U.S. history. From 2016 to 2024, he taught social studies full time with courses such as General Economics, U.S. Government, U.S. History, AP U.S. History, World History and 20th Century Conflicts. Beginning in 2024, Daniel transitioned to teaching at-risk students full time through the Rural Virtual Academy of Wisconsin.

Since September 2020, Daniel has been in charge of Historical Quality Control for Frontier Media Group, a media company that operates three YouTube channels with a combined subscriber base of over 1 million. There he was specifically responsible for monitoring the accuracy of The Front, a World War II and general military history channel. Daniel's desire to learn more about the history around him and his research expertise gleaned while at Frontier Media eventually drove him to write his first book.